LOCOMOTION PAPERS   LP186

THE
CATTERICK CAMP MILITARY RAILWAY
AND THE
RICHMOND BRANCH

by

A.J. Ludlam

THE OAKWOOD PRESS

© A.J. Ludlam, 2007.
First Edition 1993
Second Enlarged Edition 2020

ISBN 978-0-85361-747-1

Printed by
Blissetts, Roslin Road, Acton W3 8DH

Inspection of troops at Richmond station in 1939. *Northern Echo*

Publisher's note: A.J. Ludlam prepared the second edition of *The Catterick Camp Military Railway* in 2007. However, it wasn't economic to reprint the book at that time, because printing had become digital and the book was was in a pre-electronic format. The book has now been digitized, and redesigned, so that the author's second edition could be made available. Unfortunately, A.J. Ludlam died in 2018 before this work could be started.

Published by
The Oakwood Press, 54-58 Mill Square, Catrine, KA5 6RD
Telephone: 01290 551122   Website: www.stenlake.co.uk

Contents

Introduction		5
One	The Richmond Branch	9
Two	Operation of the Branch Line	33
Three	The Building of Catterick Camp	49
Four	Eclipse of the Sun, 1927	55
Five	The Military Railway: the Route Described	61
Six	Catterick Military Railway Motive Power	71
Seven	Operation of the Military Railway	77
Eight	The Remains of the Military Railway	89

Appendices

One	Constructor's Locomotives	93
Two	The Armoured Trains	94
Three	Mechanical Cab Signalling System	96

Acknowledgements

The late J.W. Armstrong, Michael Back, Godfrey Croughton, John Edgington, the late Ken Hoole, G. Horsman, Hunslet Engineering, Jim Jack, Colin Judge, Sue Pitcher, J.H. Price, Peter Semmens, Roger Spencer, Stewart Squires, Colin Stegeman, Ken Taylor and special thanks to Anne King.

The Museum of Army Transport, Beverley, the NER Association, the Public Record Office, Kew, Richmondshire Museum, Richmond, and the Green Howards Museum, Richmond.

Further reading should include Ken Hoole's exhaustive description of Richmond station and its environs in his excellent book, *North East Branch Line Termini*, OPC; *History of Catterick Camp*, Lt Col. Cole; *Locomotives of the LNER*, RCTS. *Royal Airforce Scorton and its fatal link with Richmond*, Colin Stegeman, Richmond and District Civic Society 2007.

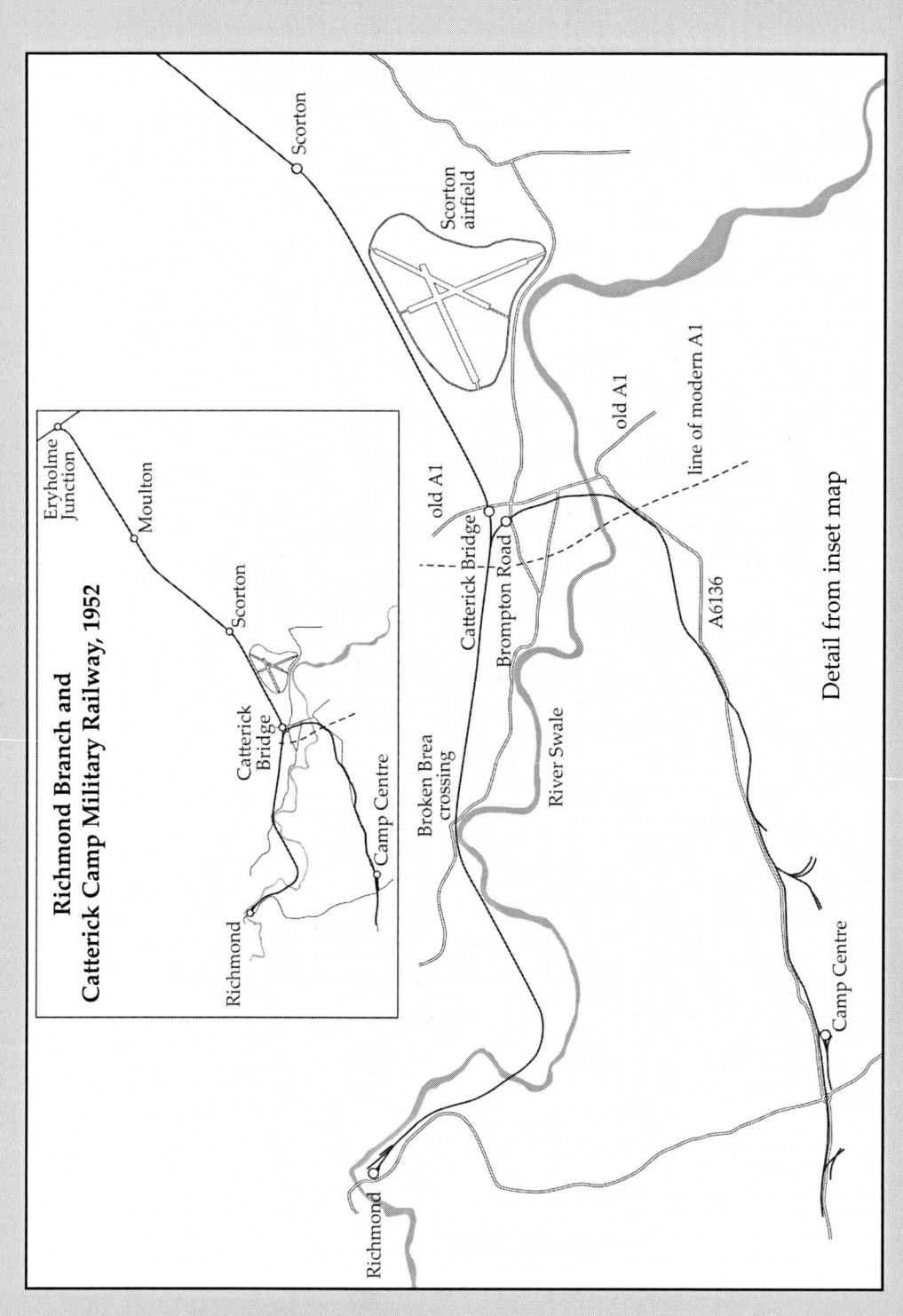

Introduction

Catterick is a place where, if you don't die at once, you will live forever.
                                Field Marshal Lord Montgomery, April 1947.

The narrowest and deepest of the North Riding of Yorkshire valleys is Swaledale; between it and Wensleydale, two miles south of Richmond, on a high open moorland, stands Catterick Camp (now Garrison), spreading out to engulf the ancient grey limestone settlements of Hipswell and Scotton and touching the outskirts of Colburn. This was once good farming country, mainly arable, and good hunting country too, the start of the best grouse moors in the North Riding.

Even before the military camp was built at Catterick the area around Richmond was the scene for summer training camps, the men attending them invariably being carried by rail. For example on 8th June, 1903, 530 militiamen from various towns in Yorkshire travelled by ordinary trains to Darlington and then by a special service to Richmond. Later they were taken by a 15-coach special, sent empty from York, to Strensall for training.

This book has been written as the result of an encouraging response to an earlier volume I wrote concerning the RAF Cranwell railway, near Sleaford, in Lincolnshire. There appears to be an increasing interest in the private railways run by the army, navy and air force, all of whom were considerable users of such lines. Like many of the light railways who operated unremunerative routes spurned by the bigger companies, and as a result, suffered almost permanent penury, the military bought second-hand stock and locomotives to operate their railways. The railway which served Catterick Camp was no exception; its coaches, locomotives and permanent way were of varying age and pedigree and yet the line was often worked by the largest engines available to, firstly the North Eastern Railway (NER), and later the London and North Eastern Railway (LNER) companies. Initially the military railway was operated in conjunction with the NER, in 1923 the LNER took over the running of the line, replacing the military stock with its own.

Any history of the Catterick Camp military railway is closely linked with the NER's Richmond branch line. Although my principal interest here is to give priority to the military railway, I have tried to give a flavour of the Richmond branch, with particular emphasis upon its connections with the Catterick Camp line.

It is perhaps worth noting that each regiment stationed at Catterick Camp is located in one or more 'lines', this term is a throw back to the days of tented camps. Thus the 1st Training Regiment Royal Signals, for example is situated in Kemmel and Loos lines. The names for the lines were adopted from locations in France made famous (or infamous) in the First World War (*see map on page 64*).

The Holiday Handbook, published by the LNER in the 1930s, describes Catterick village and Richmond within its pages:

> Catterick Bridge is and interesting spot surrounded by the finest scenery. Nearby, at the south side of the bridge over the River Swale, used to be a chapel dedicated to St Ann, where mass was celebrated daily at 11.00 am for the benefit of travellers praying for a prosperous journey.
>
> The village of Catterick, where the marriage of King Ethelbert with the daughter of Offa, the king of the Mercians, was celebrated, was a flourishing city in the time of the Saxons. It was totally distroyed during Danish raids and never recovered its former greatness.
>
> Richmond is one of the most romantic towns in the North of England. The aspect of its castle standing in its regal ruins, is eminently picturesque. Placed high on its imposing eminence, 600 feet above sea level, it overlooks not only the town and the river but a broad area of fascinating country long known as Richmondshire. There is something majestic about the aspect of Richmond Castle and little need to wonder that Turner thought it a subject worthy of his canvas. Built in 1071 the castle keep is one of the finest Norman towers in the kingdom.
>
> The original monastery of the Greyfriars was founded in about 1258 by one of the Lords of Middleham. The Greyfriars of Richmond had a bad time during the reign of Henry VIII, through the placing of St Francis before their temporal sovereign. Henry was not much given to recognising superiors either in flesh or spirit and showed his resentment by hanging and imprisoning the friars on a most liberal scale.
>
> On Whitecliffe Scar is a spot known locally as Willance's Leap, associated with a hunter whose horse leapt with him over the precipice, a distance of some 200 feet. There is a tombstone in the churchyard to the memory of Willance.
>
> One of Richmond's great treasures is the Georgian Theatre at the junction of Friars Wynd and Victoria Road. It is the most perfect example of an 18th century theatre anywhere in the world. It was built in 1788 by Samuel Butler, player-manager of one of the many theatrical companies touring England at that time. When acting ceased there in 1848 the building was used by a variety of tradesmen over the years. Its true worth was not fully appreciated until the 1930s/40s. The creation of the Georgian Theatre (Richmond)Trust in 1960 saw it restored to its original splendour.

Since the first edition was published more information and photographs have become available and are included herein.

There have been developments at Brompton-on-Swale, where the girder bridge that carried the military railway over the River Swale is part of a plan to create a new pathway. In 2005, Yorkshire Water, the owner of the structure agreed to it being used. It was seven years later that those plans came to bear, and the bridge is part of an expanding network of paths in the valley.

Richmond station building was bought from British Railways by Richmond Rural District Council in October 1972. £27,000 was spent renovating the building during 1974 and it was leased to a garden centre and ironmongers business. Local floods around the turn of the century damaged the bridge leading to the station and this, along with an outbreak of foot-and-mouth disease hit the business, many of whose customers were farmers, hard, and it closed.

The building stood empty for some time and there were rumours of the Council building a hotel on the site. This angered local people who set up the Richmond Station Regeneration Project with the intention of drawing down funding to develop and re-open the station. This they have successfully done.

The Richmond Building Preservation Trust now has a 999 year lease on the building. It houses a restaurant, a two-screen cinema, community meeting rooms and small business units. Also included is a heritage centre telling the history of the railway. In order to accommodate these facilities the train shed has been sympathetically extended, the size of the building is important in making it self-sufficient and financially viable. Over £2.6 million has been raised, with help from Heritage Lottery, European Funding, Yorkshire Forward, Architectural Heritage, Gunneside Estate and the David Carr Foundation.

A two-car Metro-Cammell dmu set approaches Richmond station with the 4.00 pm Darlington service. The River Swale can be seen to the left of the unit.   *John Boyes*

Poster announcing the opening of the Richmond branch (1846). *Author's collection*

Class 'L1' 2-6-4T No 67742 approaches Richmond station with a passenger train from Darlington in the 1950s. Built to a Thompson design by the North British Locomotive Co. in November 1948, No. 67742 was one of the last of a class of 99 engines to be withdrawn in December 1962. It arrived new at Darlington for use on services to Saltburn, Tow Law, Richmond and Catterick Camp. On Monday morning trains left Darlington for Catterick Camp at 2.55 am. 4.02 am and 5.20 am. The 2.55 was always double-headed by two 'L1s' Each train between Catterick Bridge and Catterick Camp was worked with an 'L1' at the front and rear. On 10th July, 1957 the Royal Train was worked over the Catterick Camp branch by 'L1s' Nos 67777 and 67742. *J.W.Armstrong Trust*

Chapter One

The Richmond Branch

Although authorized by the Great North of England Railway (GNER) Act of 21st July, 1845, the double-track Richmond branch was actually opened in September 1846, by the York and Newcastle Railway, the name adopted when the GNER, running from York to Darlington, was formally leased on 27th July, 1846, by the Newcastle and Darlington Junction Railway (NDJR) which ran from Darlington to Gateshead. The Richmond line was one of the shortest branches in the north-eastern region of England.

One of the principal reasons for the construction of the line was the lead mining industry in Swaledale which was highly productive at this time. It is surprising, therefore, that the line terminated at Richmond and did not continue further up the valley. As it was, the nearest mines were several miles beyond Richmond in the Hurst-Marske-Arkengarthdale area. Previously the railhead for the mining traffic was the Stockton and Darlington, Croft branch, of 1829. This was superseded by the opening of the York line in 1841, when Cowton was brought into use.

Several plans for extending the branch beyond Richmond were proposed.

The Richmond and Reeth Railway Company obtained an Act on 26th July, 1869, to construct a 10½ mile line but support was not forthcoming.

Pigs of lead being weighed and recorded in Richmond station yard before being loaded into railway wagons, a NER porter is in attendance, c.1870. *Author's collection*

A similar proposal fell by the wayside in 1895 and it was not until 1911 that the Swaledale Light Railway (SLR), taking advantage of the 1896 Light Railway Act, was approved. An agreement between the North Eastern Railway and the SLR was approved in January 1912, but support for the line was insufficient to make a start before the First World War. By 1922 the application was listed as 'Removed from list'. This would have been an interesting line, following the south side of the River Swale for the first two miles, then crossing the river near Willances Leap, continuing through Marske, to terminate at either Grinton or Fremington just before the climb to Reeth. The stillborn scheme was marked by a few surveyor's pegs in Billy Bank woods.

As the NDJR had controlled the GNER since August 1845, it was the former company that awarded the contracts for the building of the line and stations. The tender of Roberts, Elwin and Jeffrey, of Darlington was accepted for the construction of the coal depot, weigh house, engine shed and warehouse at Richmond, the stations and coal depots at Catterick Bridge, Scorton and Moulton, the station at Eryholme Junction and the gatehouse at Broken Brea, at a cost of £10,300.

Darlington Bank Top station, with its clock tower, stands at the head of Victoria Street and was built in 1877, replacing an earlier station on the same site. The station was built on loops off the main line, allowing trains not stopping at Darlington to pass outside the east wall without the severe speed restriction necessary to enter the platforms. The station was laid out in the form of an island, with bays let in at each end, those at the south accommodating Richmond and Saltburn branch trains, and those at the north trains heading over the former Stockton & Darlington

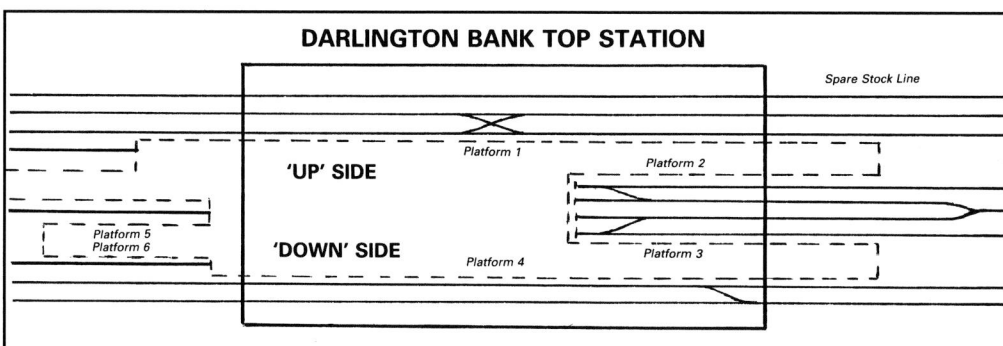

Platform 2 was used for the Richmond branch. In the late 1950s, a through Bishop Auckland to Richmond dmu used the south end of Platform 1. This connected with the 3.05 pm 'Queen of Scots' express for Ripon, Leeds and Kings Cross. The Pullman used the crossover beside Platform 1 and was the only passenger train to do so.

THE RICHMOND BRANCH 11

Darlington Bank Top station under construction in 1876. *K. Taylor collection*

The superb curved interior of Bank Top station seen here in 1877. *K. Taylor collection*

lines to Crook, Kirkby Stephen and Penrith. The outer faces accommodated main lines, but, in busy times, the central crossover allowed two trains to be handled at one platform, so that the convenient connections could be made.

Until 1975 the old Stockton & Darlington locomotives *Locomotion* and *Derwent* stood on a plinth at the buffer stops end of the southern bays. Both engines are now displayed at the North Road Station Museum, a building converted from the Stockton & Darlington station of 1842.

Bank Top's overall roof is made up of three 60-foot spans, the outer ones are 1,000 feet long. The centre span is divided by station buildings.

The Richmond line left the East Coast main line at Eryholme Junction, known as Dalton Junction until 1st May, 1901. The junction was situated in a wild and desolate place, with no proper road access to the four railway houses nearby; indeed it was not until the early 1960s that a road was made up to the Scorton – Yarm road ¾ mile away. The station buildings, like all others on the branch, were of substantial stone construction, all were designed by G.T. Andrews of York. Prior to the closing of the station on 1st October, 1911, there were up and down main line platforms, branch line trains using the western face of the down platform. A short wooden platform was used when changing for the south from the Richmond direction; passengers were carefully shepherded over the two Richmond tracks and the main line to reach the up side.

The original signal box was at the north end of the platform on the up side, this was replaced on the 1st June, 1939 by another box at the north end, but on the down side. From here at the top of Dalton Bank trains could be seen from as far away as Cowton. The signalman would push an electric bell plunger when down trains passed through, this rang a bell at Darlington station, one ring indicating a non-stop train, two that the train would call at platform 4 or terminate there. There was a down lay-by siding on the Richmond branch, its equivalent on the up side being just north of the signal box.

In the early days branch line trains terminated at Eryholme but after closure of the station trains ran through to Darlington. This brought Croft Spa into the Richmond service and at one time this became the interchange point when the Eryholme station was closed. Croft Spa is a small village on the Yorkshire bank of the River Tees and from the train the church where Charles Dodgson's (Lewis Caroll) father was Rector can be seen. The station was on the other side of the Tees, in county Durham, it was called simply 'Croft' until 1896 when it was renamed 'Croft Spa'. There were no goods facilities at the station only horse

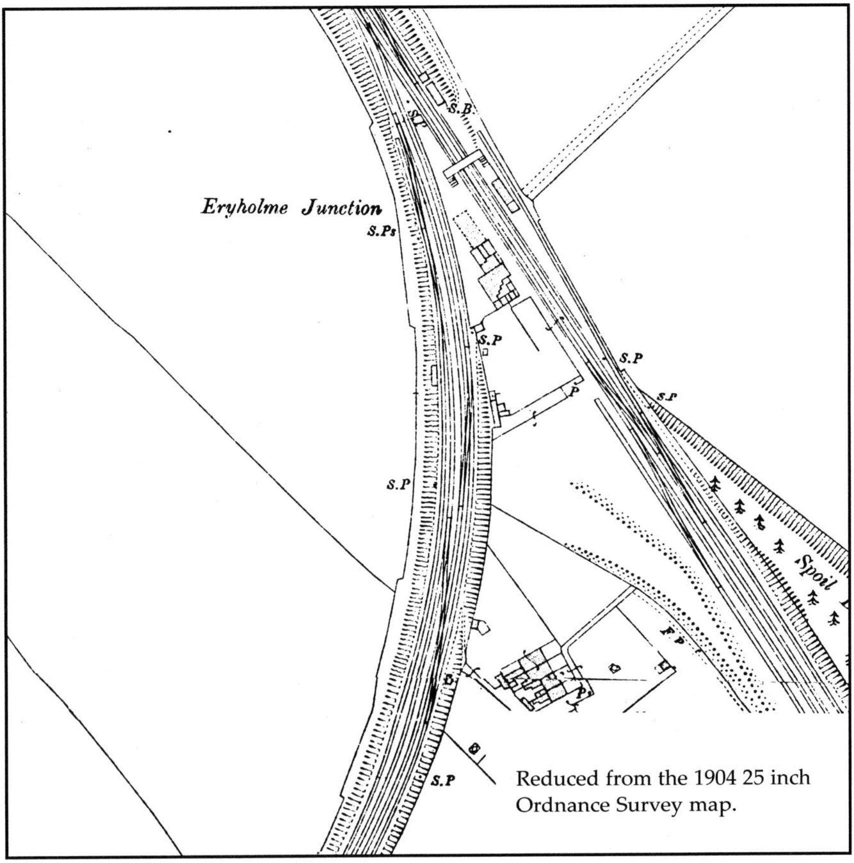

Reduced from the 1904 25 inch Ordnance Survey map.

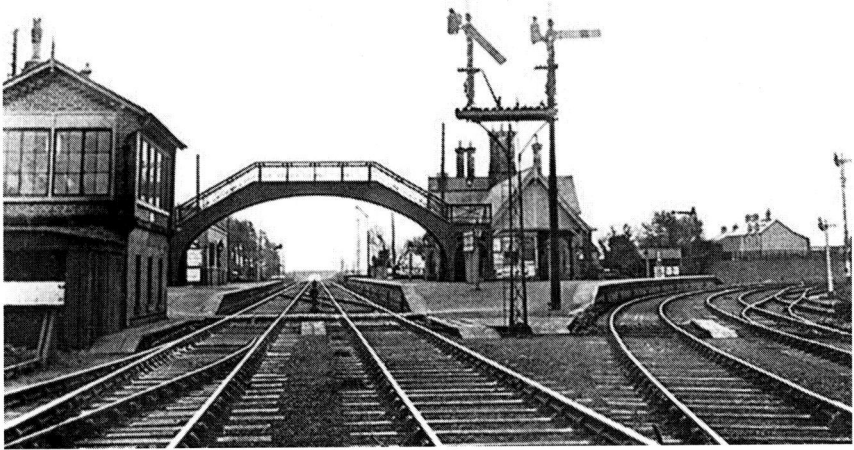

The north-end of Eryholme Junction photographed prior to 1911. The signal box was replaced in 1939, by a new box standing at the end of the island platform. The Richmond branch line curves off to the right. *Author's collection*

Class 'J24' 0-6-0 No. 1824 with a breakdown train at Eryholme Junction in June 1930. The Richmond branch turnout can just be seen to the rear of the train.   *R.A.S. Marketing*

Eryholme Junction signal box and station buildings, the Richmond branch platform (long after closure) and track are on the right, photographed on 3rd September, 1956.
R.M. Casserley

loading docks. The NER signal box was a tall structure giving a view over the road bridge which spans the line at the south end of the layout. Just before the First World War it was replaced by a low wooden box south of the bridge. This stretch of main line was the first to see automatic colour light signals of the approach-lit type, which were introduced between Eryholme and Black Bank on 12th February, 1928. Croft Spa box was retained but reduced in status to a ground frame, opening only when necessary to operate the crossover and loading dock points, on such occasions the relevant colour light signals were manually controlled.

These early colour-light signals were of the three-aspect type, battery lit by six-volt bulbs. In 1939 they were replaces by modern four-aspect 'searchlight' signals as part of the Eryholme and Darlington South resignalling programme.

As the Richmond branch left the main line it passed the works of the Darlington Rolling Stock Company, where wagon repairs were carried out. Short 45 ft-long rails announced the end of the main line and the beginning of the branch. Ancient Southern Division semaphores, and crossings sporting flat board signals with rotating posts amplified the difference further. Upper quadrant signals did not appear on the line until well after the Second World War.

Class 'G5' 0-4-4T No. 468 with a Richmond train at Croft Spa in July 1920. The engine, in green livery has a bracket behind the front coupling for the Raven electric cab signalling apparatus used on the Richmond branch. *R.A.S. Marketing*

The commencement of the Richmond branch showing the siding belonging to the Darlington Rolling Stock Company, where wagon repairs were carried out.   *P.B. Booth*

Moulton station on 9th September, 1967, looking in the direction of Eryholme Junction. The decorative gable ends on the station building are characteristic of the architecture on the branch.   *N.D. Munday*

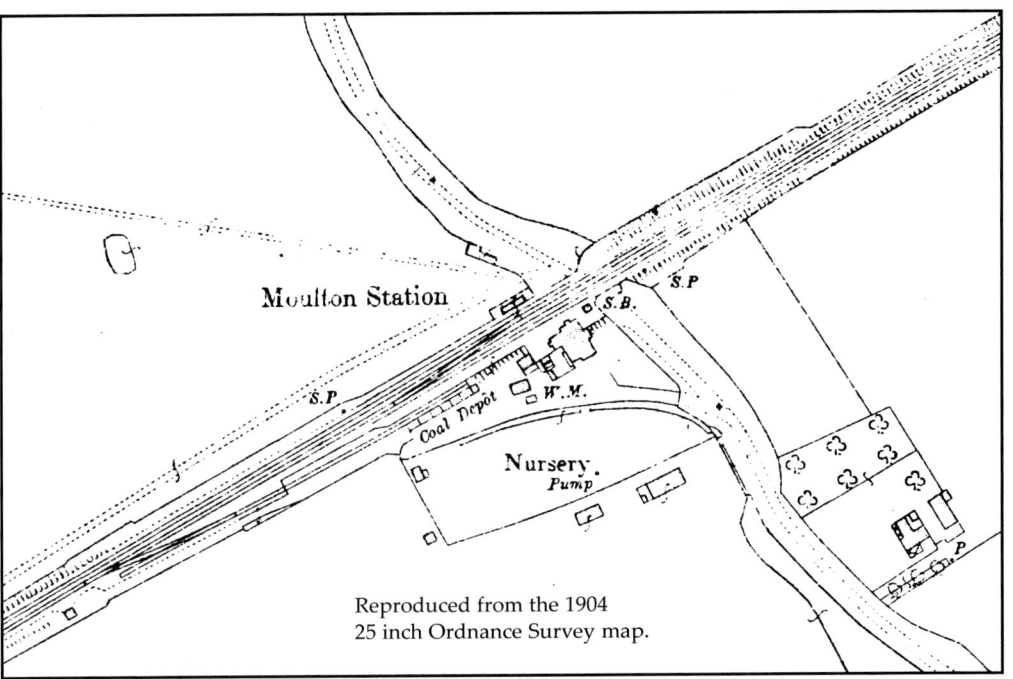

Reproduced from the 1904 25 inch Ordnance Survey map.

The first station on the branch was at Moulton, which had a ground frame and was a block post; it was demoted to an unstaffed halt on 1st October, 1956. Moulton, 2 miles 24 chains from Eryholme, had the usual North Eastern Railway coal cells and small yard. J.W. Armstrong recalled an amusing incident concerned with the name of the station:

> After Nationalisation a friend of mine was station master at Moulton. a dapper little chap who was, in the normal way. measured for a new uniform. After a fair wait this duly arrived but was obviously made for someone the size of Oliver Hardy. After much letter writing and telephoning it transpired that a station master at Moulton on the old Midland and Great Northern Line was not too happy with his uniform, exchanges were duly made and trains began running normally again.

Approximately 1 ¼ miles beyond Moulton station there was a siding serving some brickworks owned by Mr Lee. The siding was opened in 1883 but the brickworks closed in 1895. In 1897 the siding was taken over by George Lambert and Sons, closing a few years later. Reopening took place in 1919 under the ownership of J.W. Pearce, trading as the Scorton Brick and Tile Works. A signal box was opened to control the siding, this

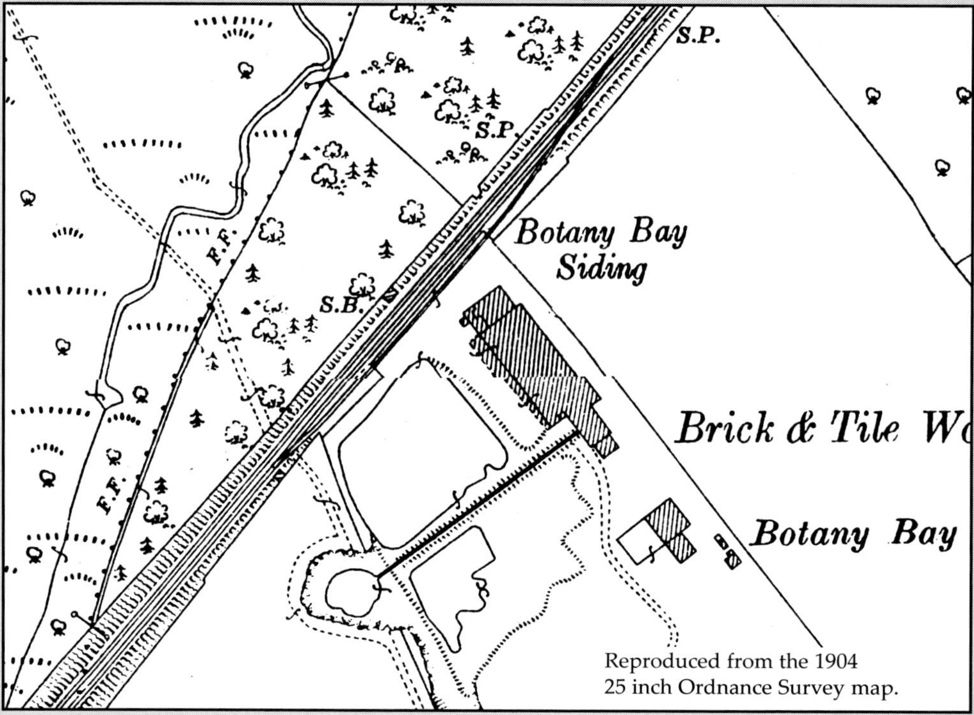

Reproduced from the 1904
25 inch Ordnance Survey map.

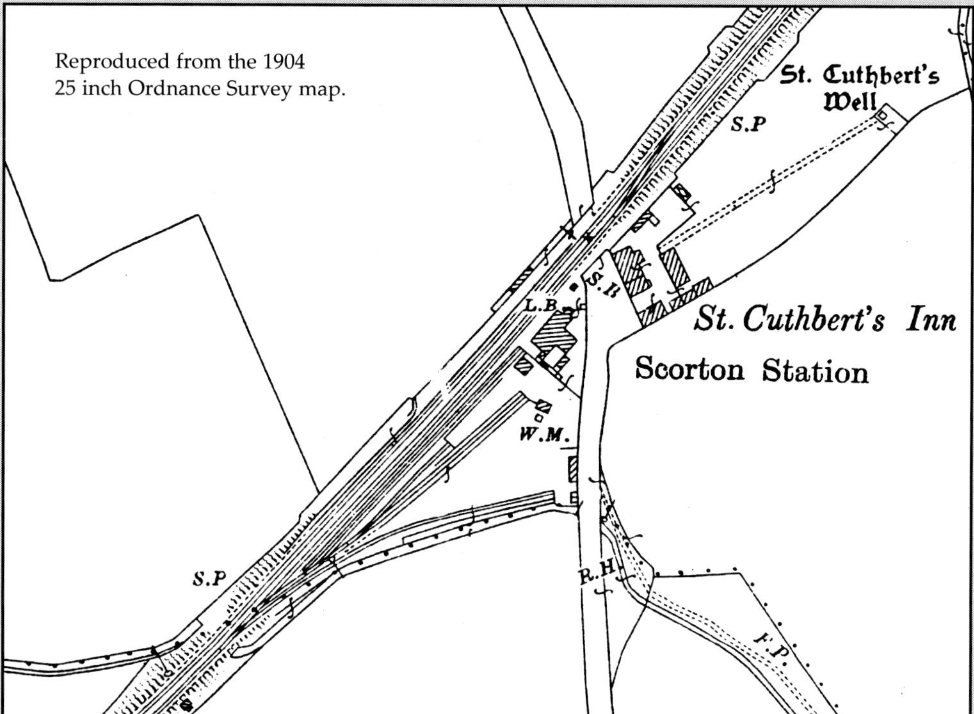

Reproduced from the 1904
25 inch Ordnance Survey map.

had the somewhat exotic name of Botany Bay and was listed in the Working Timetable until about 1930 as, 'closed except when up goods requires to work brickworks sidings'; by this time it had been deleted from the official list of sidings.

The station building at Scorton, 4 miles 38 chains along the line was, as at Moulton, on the down side of the line and similar in layout to the latter. The town of Scorton was about a mile south of the station, and had a famous grammar school and Hospital of St John of God. The station became an unstaffed halt on 2nd August, 1965.

219 Squadron was based at RAF Scorton, which was located alongside the Richmond branch line, in late 1942. Its crest was appropriate to a night fighting squadron, the death's head moth and the motto 'From Dusk to Dawn'. The squadron was equipped with the Beaufighter VIf a nightfighter aircraft. The Beaufighter, a development of the Beaufort, was designed and built by the Bristol Aircraft Company. The pilot was accommodated towards the nose, with good visibility. The navigator was in a separate cockpit to the rear. It was heavily armed with four fixed 20 mm cannon in the fuselage and six .303 machine guns in the wings. The aircraft had two Bristol Hercules air cooled 14 cylinder, sleeve-valve radial engines, each capable of developing 1,670 horse power and turning three bladed propellers some 12 feet in diameter. It was certainly awsome in terms of fire power and was said by crews to 'have the acceleration of a scalded cat.'

A view of a very neat looking Scorton station with the ground frame in evidence on 3rd September, 1956. *R.M. Casserley*

At 8.30 pm on Monday 14th December, 1942, a Beaufighter Mark VIf No. V8452, took off from RAF Scorton. On board were the pilot Flight Lieutenant Bill Hunt and the navigator/ radio location operator Flight Sergeant Harold Gysel. They were flying one of four Beaufighters which had been scrambled – their mission to seek out and intercept Luftwaffe raiders who were responsible for at least four deaths and many injuries that night. The last words the Scorton flight controller heard was Bill Hunt saying, 'I cannot control this aircraft', soon after the undercarriage had been lifted.

The Beaufighter just missed the flagpole atop Richmond Castle. The low flying aircraft was seen over the town with flames issuing from its engine exhausts, the plane itself was not on fire. The Bristol Hercules radial engine was known for its exhaust flames particularly when on full boost. Bill Hunt's difficulties were caused by the fact that a canvas weather cover had not been removed from the aircraft's tail prior to take off. He was grappling with the controls and, finding that the rudder and elevators were not responding, tried to turn back to the airfield by increasing the revolutions of one of the engines whilst shutting down the other. The plane flew towards Quaker Lane and the hillside of Bolton Crofts where it crashed having been airborne for less than five minutes.

The plane burst into flame on impact and shortly after rescuers began to arrive at the crash site. It is likely that the airmen had died on impact, undeterred by this possibility attempts were made to save the crew, but these were thwarted by burning fuel and exploding ammunition. Once the fire brigade arrived the fire was put out, allowing the bodies of the men to be found.

The most important intermediate station on the branch was Catterick Bridge, 6 miles 23 chains out, and sited where the Richmond branch crossed the old Great North Road. The station's importance increased significantly with the development of Catterick Camp during the First World War and the camp's subsequent growth during the Second World War. The military railway serving the camp, the main concern of this book, left the Richmond branch here.

The Richmond branch continued by crossing the Great North Road on the level, signals and gates being controlled from an early type of Southern Division signal box. This was the beginning of Swaledale proper, the River Swale being just to the south of the line.

Near Broken Brea crossing the line was almost at the water's edge, here it made a sweep to the north-west round Easby woods passing a siding and coal depot serving nearby Easby Hall. The siding on the up

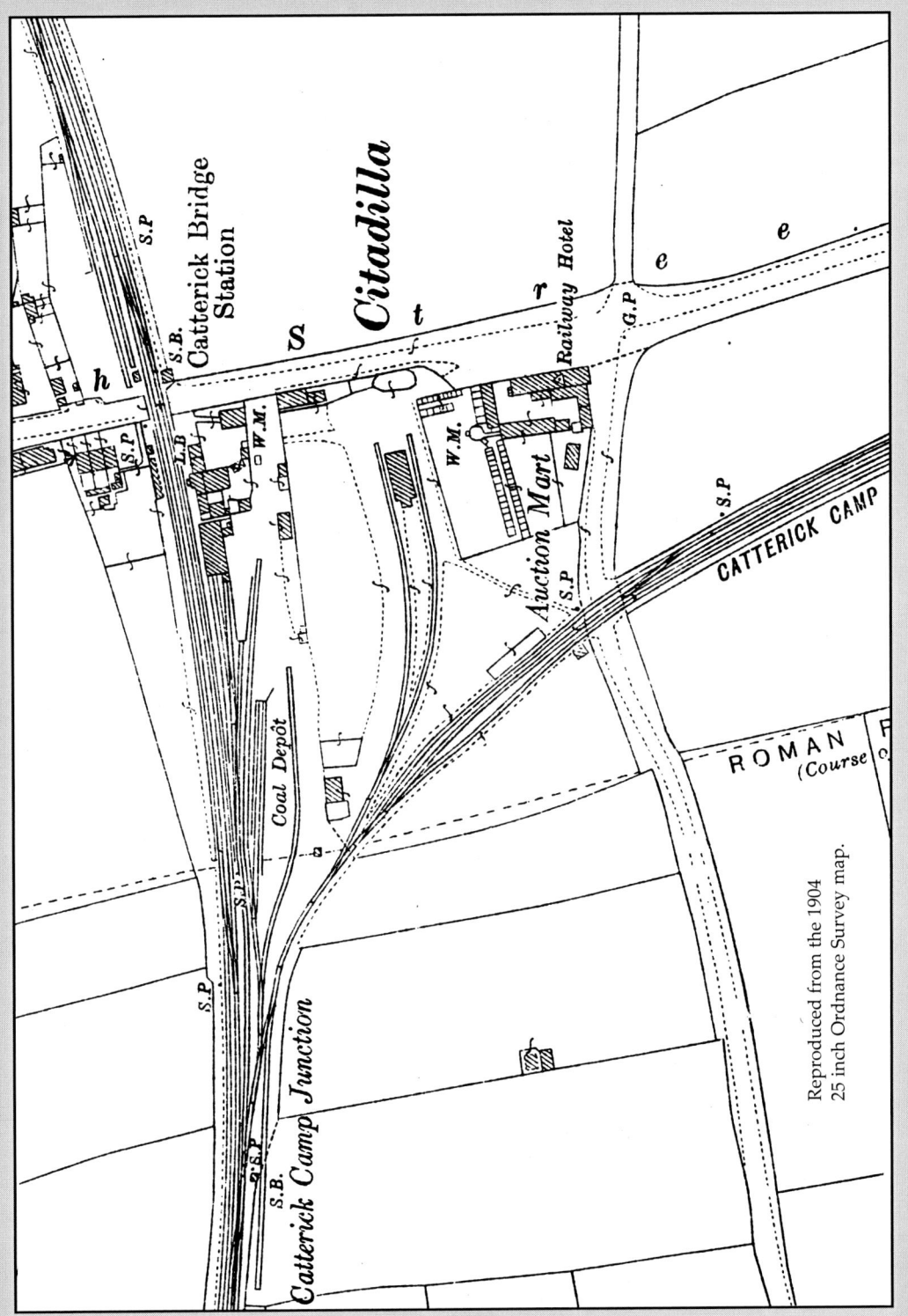

Damage at Catterick Bridge station caused by ammunition exploding in a nearby goods wagon, in February 1944. Signalman Fred Robertson was injured by flying glass.

K.L. Taylor collection

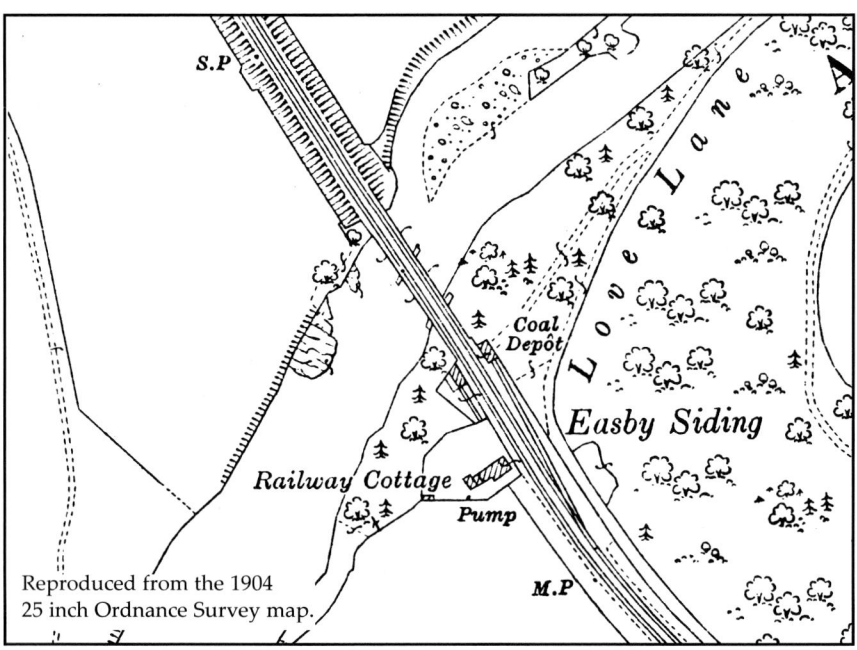

Reproduced from the 1904 25 inch Ordnance Survey map.

side, was once used by 'Mr Jaques, Gentleman, of Easby Hall, and his tenants for coal and the occasional wagon of manure'.

Just before St Martin's private crossing, a bridge carried the line over the river, about half a mile south-east of Richmond station. From here water was pumped to the tank at the station. The pump had an 8 inch diameter piston with a 10 inch stroke and was driven by a Carrick and Wardale vertical steam engine. Steam was supplied by a vertical boiler with a working pressure of 70 psi with one Friedman injector which had the reputation of being 'skittish' in its operational behaviour. The steam pump engine was tended by Bert Russell who also looked after the branch engine. Payment for the job in 1918 amounted to 24 shillings for a 53 hour week with no paid holidays.

Around another curve alongside the river and the line entered Richmond station, 9 miles 62 chains from Eryholme Junction. It was a handsome station with its roofed train shed, goods shed, two-road locomotive depot and gas works, sometimes referred to as the pump house. One of the engine shed's roads was a through road, giving access to the coal depot. There was a 45 ft turntable, situated on an outside line near the engine shed. In April 1877 a request was made for a replacement for the original, reportedly worn out, turntable. The decision was taken to work the branch with tank engines rather than replace the turntable. This decision was rescinded a few years later and

A general view of Richmond station and yard. The goods shed stands to the right of the platform, the engine shed, centre right and the gasworks in front of that.

W.A. Camwell

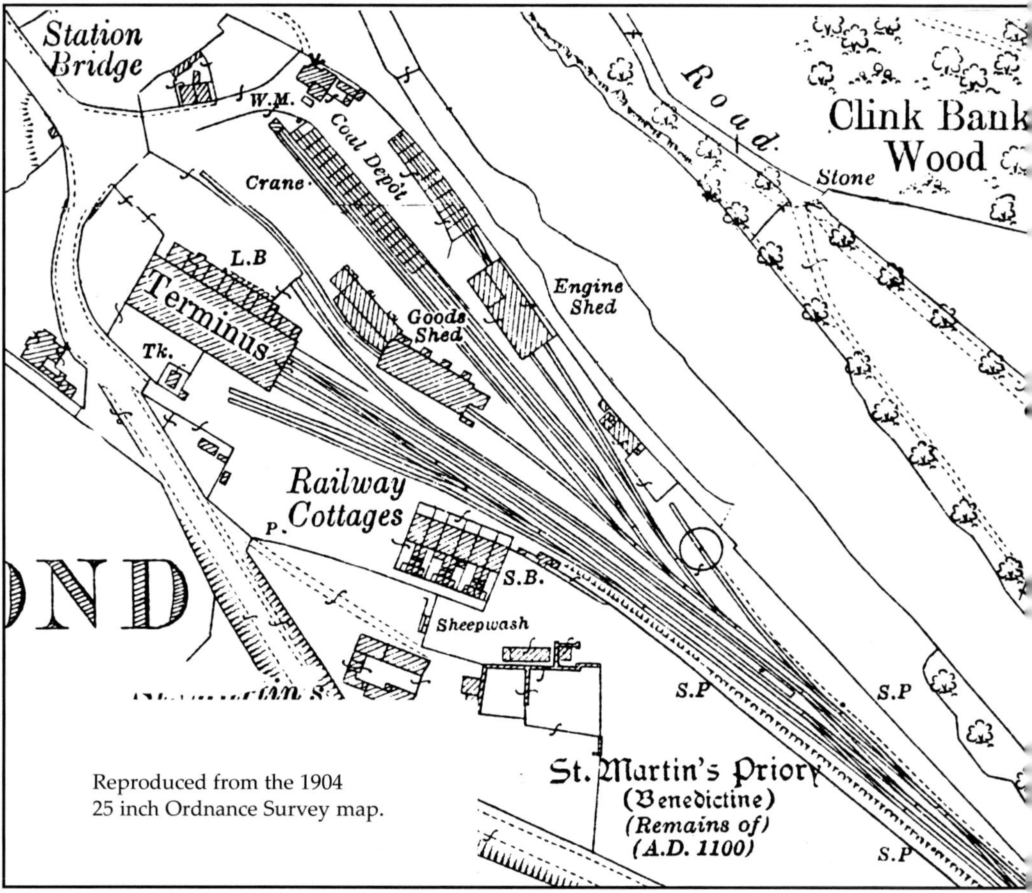

Reproduced from the 1904
25 inch Ordnance Survey map.

Worsdell 0-4-4T No. 1334 with NER clerestory stock, on the 5.20 pm Richmond to Darlington train at Richmond station on 2nd May, 1937. Note the chocks for securing the siding nearest the camera. *J. Kite*

a new I'Anson turntable was installed. The establishment at Richmond was completed by the station master's house close by the station, the depot manager's house situated at the entrance to the coal yard and a row of six railway cottages to the south-east of the station. When the York architect, G.T. Andrews, designed the station, he took particular account of its scenic location. The station, built in 1846, was in the Gothic style with an open porte cochère at the entrance and completed by a two-span train shed.

The platform was originally built low but was wide enough for the height of the leading edge to be increased later by back sloping the platform surface towards the buildings. The platform was extended in 1860 and again in 1892, these alterations could clearly be seen. At the end of the platform stood a lattice type signal gantry and a water column. The original platform and two sidings were partly covered by a glass roof, the sidings often used to house NER horse boxes hired out to local trainers for their racehorses. Often the boxes displayed the name of the hirer and the home station in gold lettering on the door panel.

The entrance to Richmond station in the early 1950s. The open porte cochère entrance is seen to good advantage. The entrance door is behind the butress to the right of the notice board. It is possible that the door in the centre replaced a window in 1913 when the booking office was altered. *J.W. Armstrong Trust*

A signal box of the early type of the NER Southern Division architecture was sited on the south side of the line close by the railway cottages. A siding known as the 'lead hole', was a permanent reminder of the early importance of the lead mining industry.

Outside the station wall was an extensive layout of sidings used for loading timber led down by three huge horses. A firm from Sedgefield loaded many tons of timber here.

The site of the station had no access road and so it was necessary for the railway company to construct a four-arch bridge across the River Swale. For 70 years the road over the bridge served only the station but with the building of the Catterick Camp a link was made with the Richmond to Catterick road. The bridge, known simply as Station Bridge, was renamed Mercury Bridge in 1975, in recognition of the long association between the town of Richmond and the Royal Corps of Signals whose headquarters are at Blandford Camp in Dorset.

The railway company also owned the road beyond the bridge up past the church to the junction of the Low Channel and Frenchgate where there were two houses for railway employees.

The terrace of six railway cottages at Richmond station with their more than substantial chimneys. The signal box coal store is to the left of the gradient post. The cottages are still standing. *J.W. Armstrong Trust*

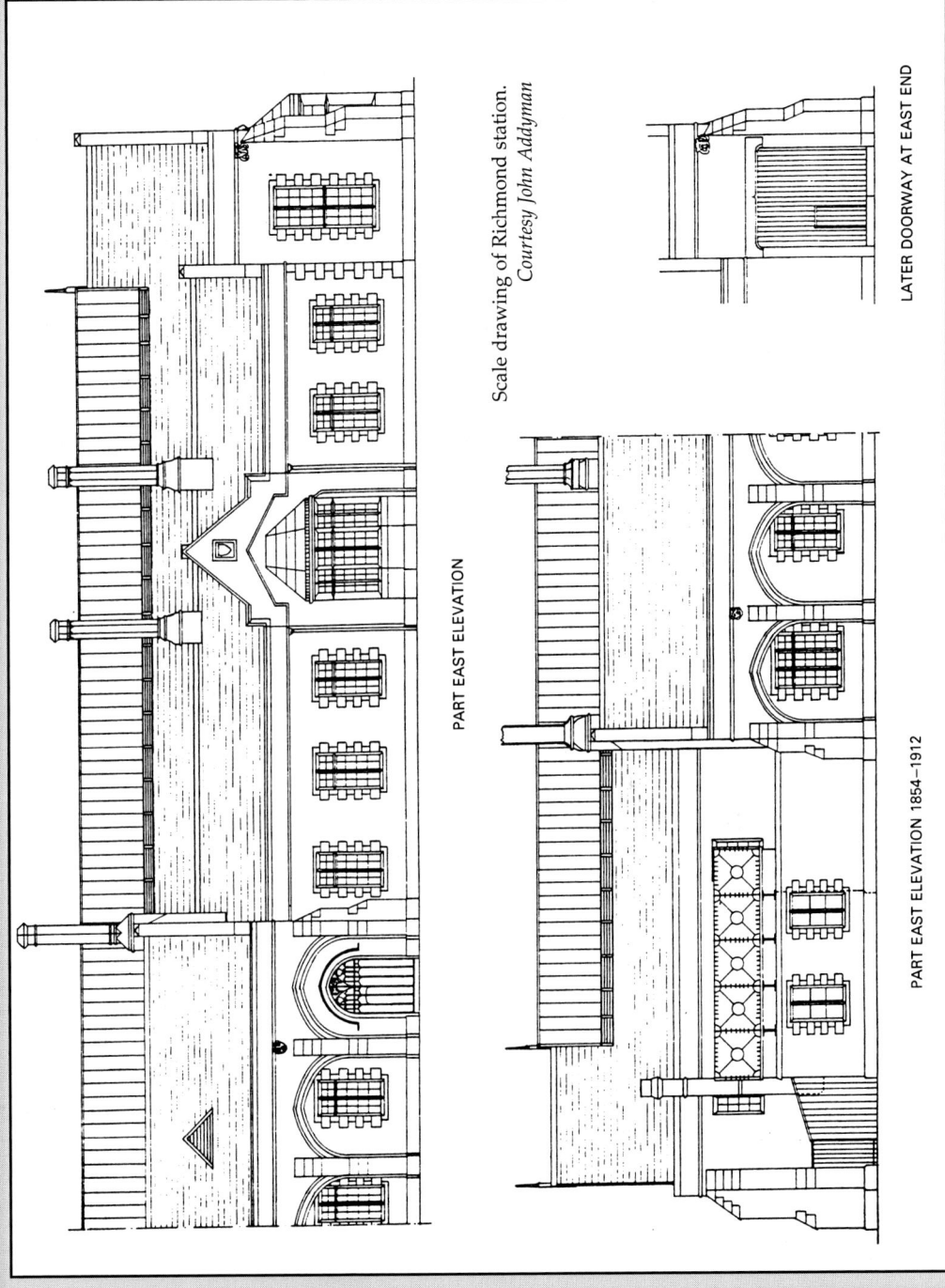

Scale drawing of Richmond station. *Courtesy John Addyman*

LATER DOORWAY AT EAST END

PART EAST ELEVATION

PART EAST ELEVATION 1854–1912

Richmond signal box was a variation of the old standard type NER Southern Division box and was extended at the turn of the century, at which time the continuous front window was installed. *L. Ward*

Cattle being loaded into wagons at Richmond station in 1945. This is one of a set of over 100 photographs commissioned by the British Council to give a comprehensive view of an English market town of that period. *J. Allen Cash*

THE RICHMOND BRANCH

The view from the platform-end at Richmond showing the signal gantry and water column.
L. Ward

A good view of the attractive trainshed at Richmond with a plentiful collection of goods vans in the sidings beyond the platform.
J.W.Armstrong Trust

The 1846-built goods shed at Richmond was built to a standard G.T.Andrews, design except that the doors in the east elevation were eight feet wide instead of the more common 10 feet. *J.W. Armstrong Trust*

The engine shed at Richmond. Until about 1950 both doorways were arch topped. Beyond the shed is part of Clink Bank Wood and part of the town on the hill beyond.
J.W.Armstrong Trust

The engine shed at Richmond showing the sqare-topped entrance that replaced an arch-topped one in about 1950.The sign to the right of the building warns, 'Beware of shunting operations'. Some of the sleepers for what used to be the second road into the shed can be seen in the foreground, left.The doorway was widened to 15 ft to make safer access to the coal cells beyond the shed. *J,W.Armstrong Trust.*

The coal cells at Richmond with the grain warehouse beyond with a delightful large-wheeled barrow parked against the wall. *J.W.Armstrong Trust*

The Gashouse at Richmond was built in 1846 – a tall chimney once stood to the immediate left of the building (*see page 23*). A modern prefabricated bulding stands alongside.
J.W.Armstrong Trust

Richmond goods shed and grain warehouse is seen to the left and the engine shed to the right. Note the mobile crane in front of the engine shed and the platelayers trolley reared up against the end of the wagon on the left. *J.W.Armstrong Trust.*

Chapter Two

Operation of the Branch Line

The branch opened to the public on Thursday, 10th September, 1846, with a service of three trains a day from Richmond to Darlington, at 7.15, 11.30 am and 3.45 pm, and from Darlington at 7.20 am, 1.00 and 6.00 pm. All trains were allowed 45 minutes for the journey except for the first train from Richmond which was timed to reach Darlington in 35 minutes. The timetable included the times of connections to and from London, York and Newcastle. Within a year the service had increased to four weekday and three Sunday trains each way. Fares were 2s. 6d. first class, 1s. 6d. second and 1s. third. This was reduced later to 2s. first, 1s. 3d. second. The third class fare remained the same and a fourth class was added at 10d.

The passenger service over the years from 1870 remained pretty much the same until the First World War. In 1870 there were five trips each way on weekdays with two each way on Sundays. In 1906 the number had increased to seven each way on weekdays with Sundays remaining as before.

The First World War period saw an early morning mail train from Darlington which returned as a passenger train at 6.00 am from Richmond. There was a late Saturdays-only trip by Richmond men

A Fletcher class 'BTP' 0-4-4WT built by Neilson in 1874, the only passenger engine class designed by Fletcher during his 30 years with the NER. This type of engine worked the Richmond branch in the early days. No. 954 was rebuilt at Darlington in 1921 to class '290' 0-6-0 (LNER class 'J77'). *Author's collection*

which left at 10.10 pm, not stopping at Scorton or Moulton and arriving at Darlington at 10.39 pm. The engine ran round before the train returned to Richmond at 10.55 pm calling only at Catterick Bridge, 18 minutes being allowed for the journey which was not bad going for a little class 'O' with six or seven bogies.

Mr Armstrong recalled,

> This was one of our favourite trains to use back to Richmond, after an afternoon watching traffic at Bank Top, plus a trip to the works yard. Sometimes we saw some real fireworks on the 10.55, one such trip I well recall. It would be about October 1922, and a real rough wild night. As was my practice I had gone up to No. 2089, to have a chat with the driver, that night it was Albert Dinsdale. Albert was one of those men who should have been an express driver, he was quite a card in his way. His whole life was his engine, he composed an alphabet from A to Z describing the automatic brake control of the branch, his home made oil trimmings and oil saving ideas he had. He always wore a guard's type of hat at work and with his waxed moustache and tall regal bearing was a well-known character in the Darlington area. His first shed had been the old passenger roundhouse at North Road, he actually brought the last engine, No. 1333, over to Bank Top when the shed closed.
>
> As I climbed in the cab of No. 2089 Albert said, 'We'll be late away tonight, the 9.28 out of York whistled for assistance at Otterington and 1042 left about

Class 'G5' 0-4-4T No. 2089 on a Richmond working at Croft Spa c.1930. In black livery, the engine retains the NER class letter, 'O', on the front buffer beam and was stationed at Richmond throughout the 1920s, moving to Northallerton in December 1929. It was replaced on the branch by class 'F8' 2-4-2T No. 469. *W. Rogerson*

20 minutes since'. No. 1042 had been standing as south pilot that night with Tommy Temple in charge, at a rough guess we reckoned another hour would elapse before we could expect Tommy and the reluctant 9.28, so we settled down in the cab for a chat. Judge our surprise, therefore, when just over 35 minutes later we heard the platform down main board rattle off and in runs 1042, tank first, with a badly steaming 'Z' and 12 bogies in tow. Tommy had shot down the main line to Northallerton in about 15 minutes, crossed over, and as the York man had decided he could get her steaming by Darlington, 1042 hung on in front and showed them the way home. He uncoupled at Darlington and the York man got away alright.

The Platform Inspector came up to our engine and said, 'Now Albert, tha's about 20 behind and they're holding the Camp man at Catterick, see what tha can do'.

This was just what the doctor ordered as far as Albert was concerned. He just walked them gently out of platform 3 and I sat back in the first compartment with my watch ready. As soon as we cleared the old South Box there was a jerk, the exhaust sharpened and he gave the old girl her head. We cleared Croft in just over four minutes, Eryholme in under seven and I believe he DID just about recognise the slow over the junction, but never before or since has any old NE clerestory stock been waltzed off the main line and round the Richmond curve like we did. We blazed a trail of sparks right away to shutting off for Catterick Bridge. We stopped in just over 15 minutes from Darlington, having knocked three minutes off the timing, no mean feat when you consider the NER branch timings.

Across at the Camp station (Brompton Road) one could just make out the shape of No. 424 champing at the bit and blowing off like mad. Before our ticket collection was completed her shrill whistle could be heard like a thousand banshees, and she was tackling the one in thirty and forty grades to the camp. No. 424 was not a particularly big engine but that whistle of hers could compete with anything the Geordies ever had.

Albert Dinsdale was also in charge when class 'P3', No. 1224, had its moment of glory one morning in 1919. By this time the goods traffic had grown heavy enough to warrant the use of 'P3's and No. 1224 was a regular visitor to Richmond. When he booked on Albert found the branch engine, No. 2089, not fit to take out the 7.45 am. He contacted the Richmond station master who arranged with Catterick Bridge to release No. 1224 from her pick-up goods duties (she was shunting at Catterick Bridge at the time on her way to Richmond) and send her light engine to Richmond. She arrived, turned and left about five minutes late with a porter in the van to help with the handbrake. Time was kept to Catterick Bridge where Albert smartly uncoupled, ran forward, and changed onto No. 468, which had been taken off the first down train. Backing onto the train from Richmond he was away and only a few minutes late at Bank Top where all booked connections were made. No. 1224, left at Catterick

Perhaps the earliest photograph known of the Richmond train shed, showing a 2-2-2 locomotive No. 69 photographed in the 1870s. Note the short length of the original platform.
Author's collection

Bridge, crossed over to the down line and took the down passenger train to Richmond. The return working was with No. 81, sent light engine from Darlington. After its brief spell in the limelight No. 1224 returned to her normal duties.

After the closure of Eryholme station on 1st October, 1911, a midday train from Richmond to Darlington stopped on Saturdays to pick up 'Company employees' wives', for their weekly shopping trip. During the Second World War certain Richmond trains stopped at Eryholme to cater for RAF personnel stationed at a nearby airfield.

There is no certainty about the type of locomotive used to work the Richmond branch when it opened in 1846; there is, however, photographic evidence provided by Mr Walton (a well known Richmond photographer in the 1860-65 period) of 2-2-2 No. 66 with Driver Metcalfe and Guard Jefferies. Another picture shows 2-2-2 No. 69 standing at Richmond station and includes the original platform. An 0-4-2 goods engine, No. 60, was also working into Richmond at that time. No. 69 was replaced in December 1876, and No. 60 in March 1878, their numbers being transferred to 0-4-4T engines. They were replaced by Fletcher's 'BTP' class of 0-4-4WTs of which numbers 15 and 207 were well remembered. These engines probably lasted until the appearance of the Worsdell class 'A', 2-4-2T, and class 'O' 0-4-4T. As well as a passenger engine, there was a goods engine, often a class 'P', stabled at Richmond.

In LNER days class 'O' (LNER class 'G5') No. 2089, was stationed at Richmond until December 1929, at which time it was replaced by class 'A', (LNER class 'F8') No. 469. This engine was reported to have remained at Richmond until the shed closed on 30th December, 1933. From 1st May, 1933 workings to and from Richmond were taken over by Sentinel steam railcars. No. 272, *Hero*, was joined by No. 2136, *Hope*, on 22nd May, followed by No. 265, *Neptune*, on 26th May and No. 2771, *Industry*, on 8th June.

Hero left Richmond on 26th May; from the 8th June there were three railcars based at Richmond to cope with a service requiring only one. By 17th July, 1933 the service was being worked from Darlington, but the three railcars remained at Richmond, *Industry* only until 30th December, 1933, the official closing date of Richmond shed. *Neptune* was there until 19th April, 1934 and *Hope* until 7th July, 1934, according to official records.

The 1923 Engine Diagrams show all passenger trains on the branch worked by the Richmond engine with the exception of the 7.55 am from Darlington and the 9.39 am return. In the 1920s Darlington shed acquired further duties on which various classes of engines appeared: 'D23' 4-4-0, 'J21' 0-6-0, 'E5' 2-4-0, 'N9' 0-6-2T and 'H1' 4-4-4T. By 1937 the

Six-cylinder Sentinel steam railcar No. 2271, *Industry*. The type 'H' with a lightweight 4-wheel trailer is on a Richmond working near Darlington on 28th July, 1934.
W. Rogerson

Class 'E5' 2-4-0 No. 1472 on an up Richmond train near Darlington in August 1927.
R.A.S. Marketing

Class 'H1' 4-4-4T No. 1526 with a Richmond to Darlington train at Croft Spa in May 1932. Built in September 1921, No. 1526 was rebuilt to class 'A8' 4-6-2T in May 1936.
R.A.S. Marketing

Sentinel railcars were little used on the branch during the week, although the 10.22 pm Darlington to Richmond service and the Sunday services remained as railcar workings. The weekly services became incorporated into the workings of Darlington men and engines, a trip up the Richmond branch being sandwiched between a trip to Crook and one to Saltburn.

In this way several different engines appeared during the day. Engines from West Auckland, Saltburn, Middleton-in-Teesdale and Kirkby Stephen, began working to Richmond, filling in during their lay-over time at Darlington. For much of the Second World War the branch was worked by large tank engines, necessitated by the wartime increase in military traffic. Classes 'A5' and 'A8' 4-6-2Ts were most common, with class 'V1' 2-6-2Ts also in evidence. On troop specials during and after the Second World War virtually any class of large locomotive could appear. There was a Fridays-only unadvertised leave train, the 3.55 pm. Catterick Camp to Kings Cross which returned at 11.55 pm on Sunday night. The former was worked by a Darlington class 'A3' or 'V2' as far as Grantham, and was the only booked main line working for the engines which were used as main line pilots at Darlington. These trains appeared in the Summer 1950 Working Timetable and ran for about 10

Class 'A8' 4-6-2T No. 69892 with a passenger train at Richmond. No. 69892 was built in 1922 and withdrawn in November 1958. *P.B. Booth*

DARLINGTON and RICHMOND

Weekdays

DOWN

Distance from Darlington		1	2	3	4	5	6	7	8	9	10	11	12	15	19	20	22	23
M.C.		Goods B TTh SO	Goods O	PASSENGER	PASSENGER arr. dep.	PASSENGER	PASSENGER	PASSENGER	PASSENGER	PASSENGER	PASSENGER		PASSENGER	PASSENGER	PASSENGER	PASSENGER	RAIL MOTOR	
		a.m.	a.m.	a.m.	a.m. a.m.	A a.m.	A a.m.	A a.m.		p.m.	A p.m.		K p.m.	HC p.m.	p.m.	p.m.	JZ p.m.	
...	DARLINGTON	6 0	6 35	6 38	8 10 8 14	8 10	11 2	11 15 12 50		2 55	4 55		6 3	7 35	7 44	9 24	10 22	
2 48	Croft Spa	*	*	6 44	8 13 8 14	8 20	11 9	11 20 12 59		3 1	5 0		6 9	M	7 48	9 29	10 27	
5 18	Eryholme	6 17	*	6 49	8 19	10 4	11 14	11 25 *		3 5	5 5		6 13		7 53	9 33	10 36	
7 42	Moulton		*	6 54	8 23 8 28	10 16	11 29	11 34 *		3 16	5 14		6 17	7 48	7 57	9 38	10 41	
9 56	Scorton		*	7 0	8 28	10 24	11 38	11 45 1 12		3 21	5 18		6 22	7 53	9 49	9 43	10 46	
11 41	Catterick Bridge	6 40	*	7 8	8 32	10 30	11 45	* 1 20		3 25	5 22		6 26	7 57	8 5	9 9 46	10 52	
15 0	Richmond		11D	7 18	8 39					3 32	5 25		6 33	8 5		9 52		

Weekdays

UP

Distance from Richmond		1	3	6	10	13	14	16	17	18	19	20	21	22	23	24	25	26
M.C.		PASSENGER	PASSENGER	PASSENGER	PASSENGER	Goods B TTh SO	Goods D	PASSENGER	PASSENGER	PASSENGER	PASSENGER	PASSENGER	PASSENGER	PASSENGER	PASSENGER	RAIL MOTOR		
		MM a.m.	A a.m.	A HC a.m. a.m.	HC a.m.	p.m	A p.m.	A p.m.	p.m.	p.m.	p.m.	p.m.	HC p.m.	p.m.	p.m.	A HC p.m.		
...	Richmond	7 48	9 16	10 50	11 56		1 47	4 0	5 42			7 6	8 25			10 15 11 7		
3 39	Catterick Bridge	7 55	9 23	10 58 12 3	12 7	10 45	1 54	4 7	5 49			7 13	8 32			10 22 12 14		
5 24	Scorton	7 59	9 27	* *	12 12		*	4 11	5 53			7 17	8 36			10 26		
7 38	Moulton	8 4	9 32	12 12	12 12	*	2 3	4 16	5 58			7 22	8 41			10 31		
9 56	Eryholme	8 9	9 37	14 P7	12 21		2 3	4 21	6 3			7 27	8 46			10 36		
12 32	Croft Spa	8 13	9 41	12 21	12 26		2 13	4 25	6 7			7 31	8 50			10 40 11 26		
15 0	DARLINGTON	8 20	9 46	11 32 12 33	12 36	1dz1 1D	2 17	4 31	6 12			7 36	8 55			10 44 11 34		

Sundays

	1	2	3	4	5	6	7	8	9	10	11
	NO. 1 EXPRESS PARCELS	PASSENGER	RAIL MOTOR	RAIL MOTOR	RAIL MOTOR	RAIL MOTOR	RAIL MOTOR	PASSENGER	PASSENGER		
	a.m.	F a.m.	F a.m.	F p.m.	F p.m.	F p.m.	F p.m.	F p.m.	F p.m.		
DARLINGTON	6 55	8 30	11 17	1 10	3 23	4 40	6 35	8 25	10 50		
Croft Spa		8 35	11 22	1 15	3 28	4 45	6 40	8 30	...		
Eryholme	7	8 40	1 25 12			4 50	6 45	8 35 10 57			
Moulton		8 44	11 27	1 20	3 33	4 54	6 49	8 39			
Scorton		8 49	11 31	1 24	3 37	4 59	6 54	8 44			
Catterick Bridge		8 53	11 36	1 29	3 42	5 3	6 58	8 48 11 12			
Richmond	7 25	9 0	11 47	1 40	3 53	5 10	7 5	8 55 11 20			

	1	2	3	4	5	6	7	8	9	10	11
	PASSENGER	PASSENGER	RAIL MOTOR	RAIL MOTOR	RAIL MOTOR	RAIL MOTOR	RAIL MOTOR	PASSENGER	PASSENGER		
	F HC	F	F	F	F	F	F	F	F		
	a.m.	p.m.	p.m.	p.m.	p.m.	p.m.	p.m.	p.m.	p.m.		
Richmond	7 35	10 12	12 10	1 55	4 5	5 20	7 15	9 15	11 28		
Catterick Bridge	7 42	10 22	12 17	2 2	4 12	5 27	7 22	9 22	11 35		
Scorton	7 47	10 26	12 21	2 6	4 16	5 31	7 26	9 26			
Moulton	7 52	10 31	12 26	2 11	4 21	5 36	7 31	9 31			
Eryholme	7 57	10 36	12 31	2 16	4 26	5 41	7 36	9 36 11 47			
Croft Spa	8 1	10 40	12 35	2 20	4 30	5 45	7 40	9 40			
DARLINGTON	8 6	10 45	12 40	2 25	4 35	5 50	7 45	9 45 11 57			

A — "HC" to or from intermediate stations.
F — "HC" except by arrangement with District Superintendent.
J — When a trailer is not conveyed one horse box or similar vehicle (fully braked) may be attached by arrangement with D.P.M.
K — "HC" to or from Croft Spa.
M — Calls when required to set down.
MM — "HC" to or from intermediate stations except by arrangement with D.P.M.
P — Stops for Company's employees on Saturdays and runs 2 minutes later forward.

S — Class D from Moulton.
V — Return of No. 2 Down.
Y — Will only convey goods and mineral traffic for Catterick Camp Branch Railway and work as required on Camp Railway.
Z — Steam train, SO.
d — Croft Junction.
x — Arr. 9.47 a.m.
y — Arr. 10.19 a.m.

Extract from the NER, Section 7, 1932 Working Timetable relating to the branch. Note that two down and two up trains called at Eryholme on Saturdays only for company's employees use (Note P).

years. Miss Snelgrove, whose father was a Sgt Major in charge of track maintenance, and who lived with her parents in quarters in the old military hospital between 1921 and 1923, recalled,

> During the 1960s, when the line was used at weekends to take the troops on leave, it was an effort for the trains coming back up the gradients full of troops on the Sunday night. They used to keep us awake with the whistles and the noise, on arrival at Camp Centre station the train was met by taxis waiting to take the men to various parts of the camp.

Leave specials ran for a good many years after the Second World War, taking two main line engines to Richmond every Friday. The 2.22 pm empty stock from Darlington was worked by a class 'V2' 2-6-2. This left Richmond at 3.50 pm for Eryholme, running tender first; there it ran round its train and continued south with the men working to York and the engine to Grantham. The first 'V2' to visit Richmond was probably No. 4806, on 24th September, 1938. Fresh out of Darlington Works, the engine was named *The Green Howards, Alexandra, Princess of Wales's Own Regiment* by Major General H.E. Franklyn, DSO, MC, the General Officer Commanding the 5th Division, and a former officer of the Green

Fresh from Darlington Works class 'V2' No. 4806 greeted by a military band on its arrival at Richmond station for its naming ceremony, on 24th September, 1938.

Green Howards Museum

Howards. Richmond had an association with the regiment going back to the year 1782. No. 4806 was worked to Richmond for the ceremony by two men who had served in the Green Howards during the First World War. The engine continued to work in the North East until 1963, when it was transferred to Scotland, finally being withdrawn in 1965.

Roger Spencer described life at Richmond station during the Second World War:

> Richmond station was very busy during the war with military traffic but the station did not see any monetary credit for all these passengers. Most used the Government railway warrants which they exchanged for tickets at the station. These vouchers were sent to Railway Headquarters to raise charges against the Government and the station had no knowledge of the amount raised.
>
> After the war the station was in prime position to cater for the National Service recruits. Several hundred young men arrived at the station on alternate Thursdays and were taken to the camp in army transport. After about six weeks they were allowed home on leave.
>
> A number of weekend specials were introduced as the traffic was so heavy on Fridays and Saturdays. The 4.00 pm train on Friday was strengthened by additional coaches and extended to Birmingham, the 5.15 pm train was extended to Edinburgh and Glasgow. A special service was introduced from Catterick Camp station to London, King Cross, and two booking clerks from Richmond carried a portable ticket rack by taxi to the camp to issue tickets for this train. Similarly, on Saturday there was a special train to Darlington from Camp Centre station and clerks went to the camp to issue tickets. At one time the train was routed from the camp via Richmond to Darlington.
>
> The revenue obtained at weekends was considerable and changed the system of accounting at the station. Before these large amounts were generated, Richmond receipts were sent to Darlington by train. A heavy mobile cash box, shaped like a truncated pyramid, was loaded on to the morning train from Richmond. Richmond takings were sealed in a leather cash bag and put into a drawer at the top of the box. When the drawer was closed the bag fell into the bottom of the box. Catterick Bridge, Scorton, Moulton and Croft Spa stations all sent their takings in the same box. At Darlington the bags were removed and the money taken to the bank with the Darlington booking office receipts.
>
> When Richmond started collecting these large sums of money at weekends it was decided to reverse the movement of the cash box and takings from the branch stations were sent to Richmond, accounted for there and taken to the bank. Because of the large sums of money involved a night safe bag was provided and, at weekends, the takings were taken to Barclays Bank's nightsafe in Richmond. As numbers of passengers from the camp increased so did the competition. Coach firms started to run weekend services to the main centres and it became necssary for the railway to take action. Special weekend fares for members of the forces were introduced; two I remember are London, King's Cross £1 16s. 5d. and Bristol £2. These were available from Friday to Sunday night/Monday morning.

A standard NER horse box built to pattern 196. Horse boxes of this type were to be seen often at Richmond station sometimes with the owner's names inscribed in gold on the door.
Author's collection

Class 'G5' 0-4-4T No. 1786 with a passenger train for Richmond at Croft Spa in May 1929. Note the horse box next to the engine. *R.A.S. Marketing*

Built as 4-4-4Ts by Raven for the NER between 1913 and 1921, the class 'H1' were found deficient in adhesion and were rebuilt as 4-6-2Ts between 1931 and 1936 then being reclassified as 'AB'. Seen here in its original condition No. 2145 was rebuilt in 1936 and withdrawn in 1959. Both classifications of this engine worked over the Richmond and Catterick Camp lines. *Author's collection*

At the four main bank holidays, Easter, Whitsuntide, August and Christmas, special arrangements were required for the large number travelling. I saw both sides of these arrangements as I originally worked at the station and later became the Railway Camp Representative (the army called me the British Railways Liason Officer) and co-ordinated arrangements at Catterick camp Headquarters at Camp Centre. About six weeks before the bank holiday the Military Headquarters asked each regiment for an estimate of numbers travelling on leave and a summary of their destinations. I consolidated the resultant information and advised the British Rail Divisional Office at Middlesbrough the number of passengers travelling to the main towns. The BR office then arranged special trains to carry passngers from Richmond. At one time there were as many as eight special trains in one day, three to London, probably one to Bristol, one Birmingham, one Leeds and Liverpool and one each to Glasgow and Edinburgh. When the programme was agreed and train times issued I worked with the Military HQ to allocate the troops to the trains. This information was passed to the United Bus Company to arrange feeder bus services from the regiments to the station.

Meanwhile the military units were providing the station with lists of the number of tickets required to each destination. The tickets were issued and debited before being collected by an officer from the unit who was authorised to sign for them. When the tickets had been sold to the soldiers the money was brought to the station, accounted for and a receipt given. On only one occasion did an officer abscond with the money. The regiment paid the amount owed, but I did not hear what happened to the officer. On these bank holidays the station gathered large amounts of money and the night safe was used regularly. We found we could get £700 in one night safe bag and a clerk, male or female, would walk up Station Road to the bank with the bag. £700 would today be worth about £25,000 [in 2020]. Fortunately no one knew the amounts we carried up Station Road.

However, Barclays bank were not very keen on this arrangement. Firstly the night safe deposited the cash bag on the floor of the manager's office and not in a secure place. Secondly, although we could get £700 in one bag it was so tightly packed in that it was difficult to get out. The system was changed so that we had two bags and we telephoned the bank manager, who lived above the bank, before we left the station and he opened the bank door and took the bags from us. Miss Ethel Hunter, who worked with me, regularly put one or two night safe bags in her shopping bag and delivered them to the bank on her way home. Can you imagine walking up Station Road at 7.00 pm on a dark night, on your own, carrying £25,000 in your shopping bag!

On the day of departure the troops were brought to the station by the United Bus Company and there were often a few thousand in the station yard awaiting the trains. Richmond was a terminal station, so most trains came right into the station, and, after unloading the passengers, had to set back from the end of the station to release the engine so that it could be attached to the other end. The train was then shunted into the station to load with passengers. A very time consuming operation.

Standard class '3', 2-6-2T No. 82029 with a Darlington-Richmond local in 1954.
R.A.S. Marketing

For special trains a more elaborate train working system was developed, and detailed engine working was provided to reduce delays both at Richmond and on the main line to Eryholme Junction.

1. A light engine sent from Darlington to Richmond.
2. A second engine, drawing carriages for the first London train would arrive at Richmond and draw right into the station.
3. the first engine would then be attached to the outward end of the train and, when it was loaded, take it north to Eryholme Junction and onto the main line.
4. Because the train would then need to travel south another engine would have been sent to Eryholme to attach to the train and move it on its way.
5. The first engine would then wait for the next train from Richmond to take it to London.
6. Meanwhile, the second engine at Richmond would have been attached to the next London train to take it to Eryholme.

Using this method of interchanging engines a great deal of time was saved in the transfer and despatch of trains.

Class 'L1' 2-6-4T No. 67777 passes Broken Brea level crossing on the Richmond branch with a passenger train. No. 67777 was built by Robert Stephenson & Hawthorns in January 1950 and had a relatively short life being withdrawn in December 1962. A Darlington-based engine, which had the distinction of hauling the Royal Train over the Catterick Camp Military Railway in conjunction with No. 67742 on 10th July, 1957.   *J.W.Armstrong Trust.*

Train loading usually went without a hitch because of the army organisation and the discipline of the troops. Similarly the return working after the holiday brought the troops back on special trains with very few problems.

One day though there was a problem. In January 1953 there were serious floods on the East Coast of England. A warning was issued that there might be a repeat of the floods during Easter weekend. The station yard was full of troops and some had already departed when the order came that troops could be needed for flood relief on the East Coast. They were told the reason and ordered to 'about turn' and board the buses back to the units. As far as I am aware there was not a voice raised in anger, all went back in good order. Fortunately, later the order was received to stand down and the trains were rearranged and everyone went off on leave.

At the end of National Service there was a run down in the facilities available, which gradually led to the closure of the line.

After the Second World War a 4.15 pm empty stock train left Darlington for Richmond worked by a class 'B1' 4-6-0, running tender first. This then formed the 5.07 pm from Richmond to Newcastle running chimney first. By the 1950s freight trains were being worked by class 'Q6' 0-8-0, 'K1' 2-6-0, or occasionally, class 'J25' 0-6-0 engines.

The Athletic Sports and Bicycle Meet, held on Whit Mondays brought a number of excursions to Richmond. This event was held at the Cricket Field, which, was encircled by an oval running and cycle track. The meetings were part of a programme of the North Yorkshire and South Durham Cyclists' Meet, the first of which was held in 1892. On 1st June, 1903, there were excursions from Middlesbrough, Saltburn, three from Bishop Auckland and two reliefs from Darlington. The empty carriages were worked back to Darlington for servicing, returning empty later to Richmond for their back workings. The return trains left from the cattle dock sidings, requiring the hand points leading to the up main line to be clamped and the attendance of a flagman. Trains were restricted to 14 six-wheeled coaches. On the following day, there were excursions from Hartlepool, West Hartlepool, Saltburn and three from Newcastle. Excursion traffic was often in the hands of class '398', '59' and 'C' 0-6-0 engines until well after the 1923 Grouping. Two favourites were Nos. 81 and 626; the former was the first engine to be cut up at North Road after the closure of Percy Main scrapyard.

On 10th October, 1963, the North Eastern Region of British Railways gave notice of their intention to withdraw all passenger services, (except certain military trains), between Darlington and Richmond but, following objections, the proposal was found unacceptable, and the trains continued to run. A second proposal for closure was submitted on 26th January, 1968, once again objections were made, but on 11th

December, the Minister of Transport gave his consent to closure subject to the satisfactory introduction of a bus service. BR announced that passenger services to Richmond would cease from 3rd March, 1969, goods traffic having already been withdrawn on 2nd October, 1967.

Prior to the second closure application, BR had singled the line from a point 246 yards west of Catterick Bridge station to Richmond. This section was then worked under the 'one engine in steam' arrangements, thus making Richmond signal box redundant. All points were secured out of use in the normal position, pending removal. Before proceeding from Richmond station the guard had to receive assurance from the Catterick Bridge signalman that the gates at Broken Brea and Parkgate Lane level crossings were secured across the roads. In August 1968, Richmond signal box and the 1942 water column on the station platform were demolished and redundant track removed. The line between Catterick Bridge and Richmond closed completely on 3rd March, 1969.

A two-car Metro-Cammell dmu leaves Catterick Bridge station on the then single line to Richmond with the 5.36 pm service from Darlington on 21st August, 1968. The Catterick Camp Military Railway strikes off right, above the second coach of the train.

John Boyes.

Chapter Three

The Building of Catterick Camp

In 1908 Lord Baden Powell was appointed General Officer Commanding (GOC) the Northumbrian Division (Territorial Force). At this time the Divisional Headquarters was at Richmond and during his tour of duty in the area Baden Powell was called upon to survey the district with a view to the establishment of a military training centre in the north of England. When he first arrived at Richmond he stayed at 'The Kings Head' but later two cottages in the castle yard were converted into the GOC's residence. At this time the battalion clothing stores, arms and equipment of the West Yorkshire Militia were housed in the Norman keep of the castle. The Militia used to carry out their annual training at Richmond. The training was spread over two months, the first being devoted to the recruit training period, and the second saw the whole battalion assembled. The men lived under canvas on Richmond Racecourse, the officers quartered in the town. This period became known as the Richmond 'season' with dinners, balls, garden parties, and finally, a review before the Militia broke camp.

It is likely that Lord Baden Powell made recommendations to the War Office suggesting the suitability of the Catterick area as a training ground and possible permanent camp. With the outbreak of the First World War, Lord Kitchener's plan was to raise an army of 1,200,000 men, with corresponding accommodation for the same. The planning, organization and construction of this vast project was initially handled by the War Office Directorate of Fortifications and Works, later a Barrack Construction Directorate was formed to deal with such matters.

General Scott-Moncrieff travelled north to inspect Jervaulx Moors, with the intention of selecting a training area and camp near Thornton Stewart, staying with Mr J.J. Moubray at Killerby, Catterick. Mr Moubray was concerned about the prospect of a large military camp being built on good agricultural and hunting land. It was suggested that the general should look at Newfound England. This he did and from the high ground of that area he was able to see the major portion of what was to become Catterick Camp.

The area on which the camp was to be built took in the Scotton Hall Estate, owned by Mrs Stevenson, who in fact continued to live at Scotton Hall until it was purchased by the military in 1925, becoming the residence of the General Officer Commanding. Hipswell estate, the property of the Prior-Wandsworth family and parts of the D'Arcy-Hildyard family, and the Brough estate, the property of Sir Henry Lawson, were also included in the area of the camp.

The first intimation the local residents had of any land in the area being used for military purposes was a meeting between Sir Henry Lawson and two surveyors, towards the end of September 1914. Sir Henry walked from his house towards Catterick Bridge and noticed two men with theodolites, one standing on Catterick Bridge the other in Sir Henry's private carriage drive. When asked what they were doing the men replied that they were taking a special survey for a railway line, 'to run across Catterick Bridge until a proper bridge is built to carry the line to the new camp'.

'What new camp?' asked Sir Henry.

'The camp up there', was the reply, the man pointing in the direction of the site for the new camp. Sir Henry asked how they were going to take track across his carriageway. 'No difficulty there, it will come straight across here'.

Within a month construction was under way. The camp line had to climb about 700 feet in the first three miles and speed of construction was imperative. It had been decided to leave the Richmond branch at Catterick Bridge station and avoid another crossing of the Great North Road. A trailing junction was laid at the west end of the station goods yard, and the yard itself was greatly enlarged. A major obstacle was the River Swale which had to be crossed approximately half a mile from the start of the military line.

Construction teams comprised men from the newly opened ROD Corps, centred at Bordon, in Hampshire, and local railway men. To facilitate rapid construction a temporary 2 ft gauge line was laid, leaving the goods yard at Catterick Bridge and swinging slightly east of the line as it was eventually laid. The temporary line crossed the River Swale by means of the Great North Road bridge and along an embankment which rose alongside the road so as to be level with the top of the bridge. The line continued to run alongside the road to Brough Hall, turning south-west after ¾ mile and climbing steadily to the camp centre.

The motive power used to work the narrow gauge line comprised WO 4219, an 0-4-2 saddle tank built by Kerr Stuart (Works No. 1215/built 1912), delivered to Catterick in May 1915. Also, rather ironically, an 0-4-0 Orenstein Koppel well tank (686/1900); this was one of several German narrow gauge engines which appeared in the United Kingdom during the early 1900s. These two engines pounded along the narrow gauge formation conveying the loads of building material to the site of the camp until the standard gauge line opened at the end of 1915. The large depression at the north end of Catterick Racecourse was caused by excavation at the time of building the railway and the camp.

THE BUILDING OF CATTERICK CAMP 51

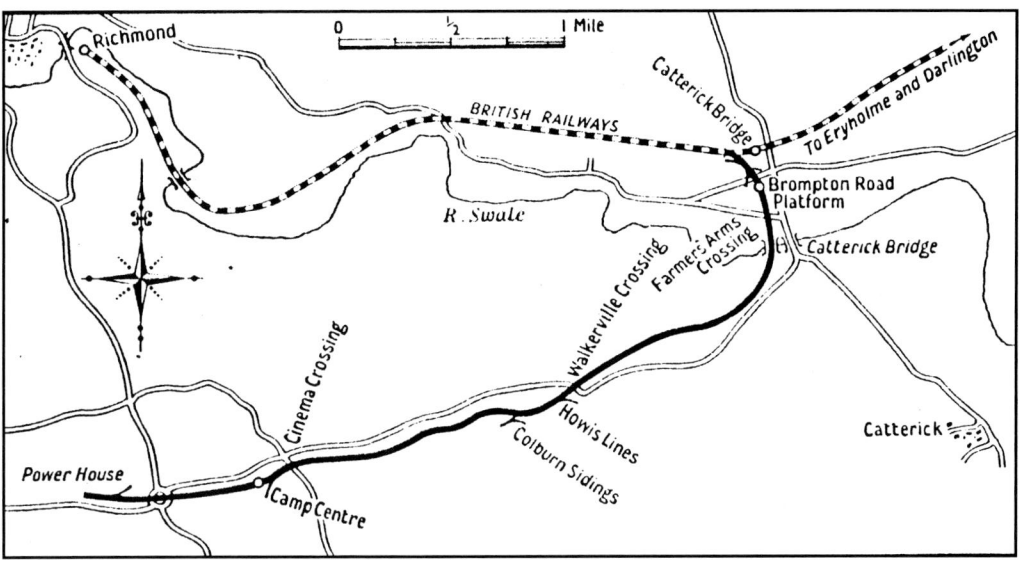

Map of the Catterick Camp including the Military Railway.

An 'Old Type' Kerr, Stuart 'Wren' class locomotive. Several of this type were used during the construction of Catterick Camp Military Railway. *Hunslet Engine Co.*

When not in use the two engines were kept in a wooden shed near the course of the old Roman road at Catterick Bridge. When they were made redundant by the new main line, they were left where they stood; the shed gradually fell to pieces around them leaving them exposed to the elements; they were cut up in 1924. Additional narrow gauge engines were used within the camp area by the construction company, Harper Brothers, these are listed in *Appendix One*.

The first loads of material for the construction of the camp arrived in the spring of 1915; the contractors drove their carts of timber and their steam rollers through standing corn and crops of roots and wheat, the lines of newly built huts taking over the farm land before the harvest could be gathered in. The camp was designed for two divisions, representing accommodation for 40,000 men and requiring some 2,000 huts. With the addition of the associated facilities such as the railway and roads, water supply, lighting and drainage, the works represented a massive undertaking. Despite this and formidable wartime difficulties, the camp was constructed in a very short time.

The Royal Engineers' Officer appointed to supervise what, at the time was described as, 'the semi-permanent camp at Catterick' was Colonel S.H. Exham, who had been involved with the building at Woolwich Arsenal, Portsmouth Dockyard and the Naval base at Rosyth. It was the 'semi-permanent' implication, contained within the original proposals, that persuaded local inhabitants to allow what they regarded as a temporary wartime measure to be built without too much fuss. If it had been realized that the measure was to become permanent there would have been considerable local opposition.

The camp was first named Richmond Camp, but this led to postal confusion with Richmond in Surrey. Kitchener Camp, was suggested, but Catterick Camp was chosen. The choice came about because the new camp was closer to Catterick village and Catterick Bridge station, and secondly in recognition of the area's earlier military associations, dating from Roman times.

St Oswald Garrison Church was built in 1915 as a temporary building. It stood at the cross roads where Richmond Road is crossed by Hipswell Road. The interior was spacious, with timbered walls and high pitched roof. Hanging from the walls were a number of Regimental and Corps flags. The very nature of the building's construction was such that, in consequence, it was demolished so quickly that many people arriving to attend morning service one Sunday found the church was gone! It was replaced by St Martin's Garrison Church.

The Officers Club was built in 1918; on the site of Pleasant Dale Farm, which stood in the camp area. The club was built by German prisoners of war in 1917/18. The funds for its construction were raised by subscription in the North Riding. It was opened 'for the use of the Officers of the Catterick Camp', on 18th June,1918 by Field Marshal HRH The Duke of Connaught.

Inside the club were the souvenirs of two Royal visits: a signed photograph, dated 1941, of HRH The Princess Royal, in the uniform of Chief Controller of the ATS, and a photo of King George Vl, in the dress of a Field Marshal and Queen Elizabeth, taken on the occasion of their visit to the camp on 28th August, 1940, the photo autographed by both the King and Queen.

The club was spacious and well-appointed with a large central hall for dining or for use as a lounge. There was a bar, snack bar, dining room overlooking the terrace, Wwriting and card rooms and a games room equipped for billiards, darts and table-tennis. A feature of this room was the murals by G.G. Giles, a Major, Royal Field Artillery. The continuous series of drawings depicted yachting, shooting, fox hunting, pig sticking, polo, steeplechasing, fishing, flying, cricket, stalking, hockey, boxing, swimming, rowing, golf, coursing and even ferreting.

The club was at the centre of social life in the camp.It was demolished in 1967.

The games room at the Sandes Soldiers Home at Catterick Camp in the 1920s.

Author's collection

In October 1916, the first soldiers arrived at the camp. The emphasis had been upon the erection of huts, rather than the building of roads and pathways, with the result that the winter weather soon turned the soft agricultural land into a rutted morass into which duckboards sank and gumboots disappeared as their owners were dragged clear. These conditions lasted for most of the wartime period. Certainly troops trained at Catterick Camp were well prepared for the conditions which obtained at Passchendaele and the Somme.

The building of the camp led to a large amount of additional traffic, not only at Catterick Bridge but also at Richmond. Some engines used in the construction of the camp were based at Richmond shed, including WD No. 104, formerly a NER class '1350' 0-6-0ST, sold out of service to the Darlington dealer J.F. Wake for £300 in 1911. This engine was repaired at Darlington Works for the War Department, returning to Richmond shed on 19th October, 1916. A NER class 'H' 0-4-0T was also thought to be at Richmond. To work these engines drivers Sharp and Sherris were transferred from Newport to Richmond. Driver Sharp had joined the NER in 1898, became a fireman in 1900 and a driver in 1914. Regular drivers and firemen based at Richmond at that time were W.M. Reed, A. Hunter, J.H. Stephenson, J. Render, J. Stabler and M. Callaghan.

A dance taking place in Richmond in 1945, part of a photographic study of Richmond carried out by the British Council.   *J. Allen Cash*

Chapter Four

Eclipse of the Sun, 1927

The last total eclipse of the sun seen in England prior to the 20th century was on 22nd May, 1724. With this thought in mind it is easy to understand the public speculation which greeted the 1927 phenomena. Place the event within the context of the period, with its largely immature road transport, and one begins to understand why three of Britain's railway companies saw the possibility of a large influx of passenger traffic.

Total eclipse of the sun can only occur at the time of a new moon, and when it does its climax the corona, with its magical flamelike effect, can only be seen from a small strip of the earth's surface, known as the total eclipse belt. Predictions for 1927 were that this belt, 30 miles wide, would strike the United Kingdom from the south-west, at such an angle across St George's Channel that Ireland and Pembrokeshire would be entirely omitted. Then, at 6.23 summertime on the morning of 29th June the great

Crowds of people pack the station platform at Leyburn, on the Wensleydale branch, waiting for their return trains after the eclipse of the sun on 29th June, 1927. The coaches on the right supplied breakfasts before and after the eclipse.   *H.C.Casserley*

shadow, or umbra, would appear over Tremadoc Bay. Speeding along at 100 miles a minute it would promptly traverse parts of Lancashire and Yorkshire before reaching the North Sea at 6.25 am. Saltburn and Ryehope would flank the area where the east coast was pierced.

No matter from where it is viewed the effect of the umbra lasts less than half-a-minute. On this occasion a likely maximum totality of 25 seconds was forecast for Hartlepool, which must have cheered the LNER enormously. All three companies must have drawn satisfaction from an additional forecast that places slightly off centre, for example Criccieth, Beddgelert, Llandulas, Southport, Settle, Richmond and Darlington would be only less marginally favoured. Even peripheral areas such as Pwllheli, Portmadoc, Colwyn Bay, Rhyl, Prestatyn and Stockton-on-Tees would suffer no greater loss than a few seconds of total darkness. The stage was set and the railway companies announced their plans to an excited public.

With Lancashire's two million population in mind the London Midland & Scottish Railway (LMS) took a firm line. Eschewing the risk of industrial pollution and obliged therefore to accept the alternative hazard of sea fog, they plumped for Southport as their 'pearl of the

Class 'D20' 4-4-0 No. 711 pilots class 'B16' 4-6-0 No. 1372 with an eclipse of the sun excursion at Leyburn, North Yorkshire on 29th June,1927. The watertower can be seen near the engine and the catering coaches in the goods shed sidings on the extreme left.

H.C.Casserley

north', with Abergele as first reserve. Three large posters were specially designed. One emphasized the merit of Southport, a shade euphemistically, as being in 'the centre of the totality band', the other posters were couched in more general terms.

Excursion trains were publicized and these converged on the Lancashire coast from many parts of the country. One restaurant car train, scheduled to leave Euston at 11.12 am on Tuesday, 28th June, reached Southport at 4.10 pm, its flat (third class) return fare of 35s. 3d. left passengers free to return, two five or eight days later. Another, tailored for busier people, left Euston at 11.10 pm on Tuesday, deposited passengers at Southport at 3.45 am and undertook to have them back in town by 1.02 pm. Such ingenuity was well rewarded, for in the event 14,000 people travelled by LMS specials. A later calculation established that on the day of the eclipse no fewer than 70,000 souls found a use for LMS transport.

Southport did rather well, the sky remained clear. At the vital moment the large crowd, already hushed as the last sliver of the sun was blotted out, felt the temperature drop sharply as the great shadow passed overhead. Conditions at Abergele were not quite so good, rain had started to fall at 5.00 am. Even then the crowd was not totally disappointed, for once again darkness suddenly descended and the lights of Rhyl, four miles distant, sprang strangely into sight.

As might be expected the Great Western Railway's (GWR) approach was almost patrician by comparison. With control of Tremadoc Bay securely under their belt possibly GWR management felt that no special pleading in the form of posters was necessary. A wide range of excursion trains was, however, duly advertised. Most centred on Criccieth. Those running from London left Paddington at varying hours between 11.10 am and 9.22 pm on the Tuesday. Eating and sleeping facilities were provided as required.

Unfortunately nature chose not to collaborate and around 3.00 am, as lengthy excursions from all parts began to roll into Criccieth, torrential rain began to fall. So wretched did conditions became that many passengers refused to leave their coaches. Brave hearts who did venture forth were soon driven to join a seething mass of wet humanity already sheltering under Criccieth's modest station roofs. Undaunted several hundred schoolboys nosed out the coal siding where the dining saloons were berthed and sank their sorrows in a hearty breakfast. Yet such is the magic of an eclipse, as zero hour approached the crowds quietened expectantly. All shunting ceased, engine whistles were silenced and a hushed expectation ensued. Alas, however, low-lying cloud saw to it

58 THE CATTERICK CAMP MILITARY RAILWAY

Gas cylinders supplying the dining coaches in the goods shed siding at Leyburn station during the total eclipse of the sun on 29th June, 1927. *H.C.Casserley*

Plan of the location of the trains on the Richmond branch for the eclipse, with trains stopped by roads leading to Richmond race course.

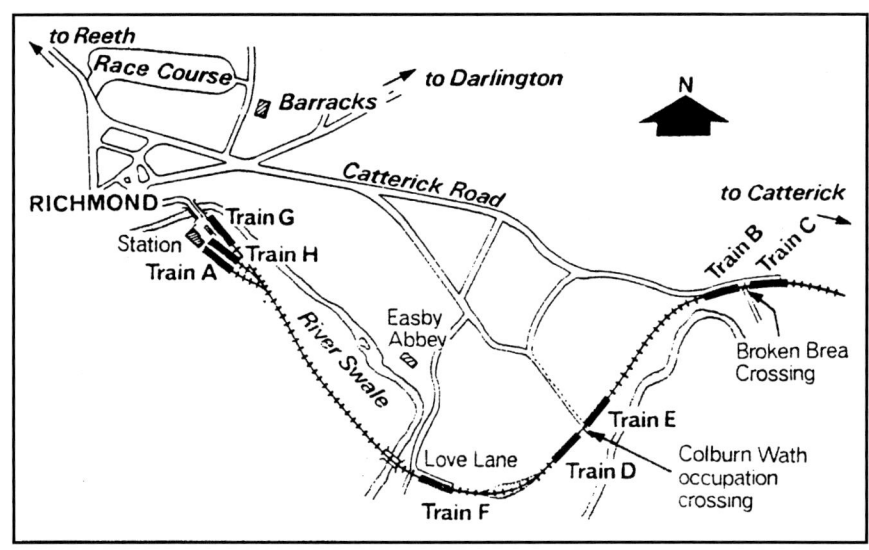

that the event which followed had little substance and a miserable shadow of sorts rewarded those who had made the long trip to the Welsh coast by GWR.

Concious of its heaven-sent geographical superiority, the LNER had the biggest fish of all to fry. They knew that on the day of the eclipse Yorkshire's Moors would resound to dialects from all over the country. Visitors would flock there , a large number from London and the south. Eating facilities, sleeping arrangements, inordinately heavy passenger traffic, the LNER was confident that King's Cross could handle it.

In the event it was the rival companies who were nearly eclipsed by the sheer magnitude of the LNER operation. At King's Cross pressures commenced at the crack of dawn on Tuesday morning for, excursions apart, hundreds of additional viewers opted to travel by ordinary express. At 10.00 am when class 'A1' Pacific No. 2558 *Tracery* took out the 'Flying Scotsman' she had 560 tons behind her. The 11.20 am absorbed eight Pullman cars, and, still going strong, the 1.15 pm was loaded to 530 tons. Next day, neatly reversing the process, the 4.30 pm express ex-Newcastle arrived at King's Cross with 565 tons.

As evening fell King's Cross' staff, hard pressed all day, now faced the most daunting task of all. No fewer than eight special trains, fully loaded, were due to be dispatched within the compass of two hours. The miracle was duly achieved, but imagine the situation in King's Cross locomotive yard as the drama shown on the table below began to unfold.

TABLE I. LNER: ECLIPSE SPECIAL TRAINS, JUNE 28, 1927

Train No.	Depart KX, p.m.	Destination	Locomotive			Gross load,
			No.	Type	Class	tons
1	7.45	Leyburn	4442	4-4-2	"C1"	240
2	8. 5	West Hartlepool	2557	4-6-2	"A1"	445
3	8.15	Richmond	4475	4-6-2	"A1"	400
4	9. 5	do	2546	4-6-2	"A1"	430
5	9.15	do	4311	4-4-0	"D3"	
			4411	4-4-2	"C1"	450
6	9.25	do	2553	4-6-2	"A1"	480
7	9.38	do	4443	4-4-2	"C1"	
			4460	4-4-2	"C1"	410
8	9.45	Croft Spa	116	2-6-0	"K3"	470

Elsewhere a further 29 specials set off that evening. A total of 16,488 passengers were thus transported by the LNER and even the last special to arrive was on the scene 31 minutes ahead of the eclipse.

Easily the most popular venues were Richmond and Leyburn. Apart from a solitary excursion from King's Cross, Leyburn also played host to special trains from Norwich and Colchester, Scarborough, Leeds, Hull,

Dewsbury and Nottingham. To cope with the abnormal circumstances an LNER control coach was set up at Leyburn station, two further coaches provided eating and sleeping facilities for staff. Old locomotive tenders and gas tank wagons supplied water and gas for restaurant cars, and, behind the station, an official saloon with a locomotive in steam stood ready to meet any emergencies.

Not far away, at Richmond, even more remarkable railway arrangements were under way. With eight early morning special trains descending on the locality the LNER had chosen to employ one of its running lines between Catterick and Richmond as a standage area. Trains were identified by alphabetical letter and passengers tickets were marked accordingly.

The diagram, *on page 58*, indicates how eight trains were parked over the two miles between Richmond station and Broken Brea levelcrossing. Equally interesting is the sequence in which the trains were scheduled to leave Richmond station for their home destinations later that morning after the eclipse, shown in the table below.

TABLE II. LNER: DEPARTURES FROM RICHMOND, JUNE 29, 1927

Train	Destination	Depart Richmond
H	Kings Lynn	7.55
A	Kings Cross	8.15
G	Edinburgh	9.15
F	Marylebone	10.45
D	Kings Cross	11.09
E	do	11.33
B	do	12.55
C	do	1.30

Richmond race course was the site chosen from which most passengers would enjoy the eclipse. Buses met trains on arrival at Richmond station and conveyed the occupants direct to the race course, where a military band and sundry other entertainment whiled away the time prior to the eclipse. For operating reasons passengers in trains B and C were obliged to have breakfast before the eclipse. The only deviation from the master plan was that passengers in train E viewed the eclipse from Barden Fell, instead of the racecourse. Immediately after the eclipse buses for trains A, H, G, F and D lined up at the racecourse entrance ready to transport passengers back to their trains for breakfast.

With breakfast over, buses attended Love Lane, Colburn Wath and Broken Brea to take passengers into Richmond, there to see such items of historical interest as train departure times permitted.

Chapter Five

The Military Railway: the Route Described

The line, laid single apart from crossing loops, contained many level crossings along its 4½ mile route; most were for the convenience of the military and local farmers, only one, Farmers Arms, being provided with gates. From Catterick Bridge· the principal crossings were at Brompton Road, Farmers Arms, Walkerville, Cinema and Camp. Each was provided with an army type telephone, and, in addition, the small hut at Farmers Arms was fitted with an instrument showing which single line tablet was out, together with a block repeating bell. The tablet instruments themselves were at the Camp Centre and Brompton Road signal boxes. Annett's keys were used to unlock the intermediate ground frames at Colburn sidings and Howis lines. Normal three-position block telegraph was in use between Brompton Road and Catterick Bridge signal boxes.

The military railway began at a trailing connection close by milepost 6½ on the down line at the Richmond end of Catterick Bridge station. The same connection gave access to a small goods yard where coal for the camp was transferred to lorries. A small ground frame controlled movements to and from the camp railway and the goods yard. All trains on the line working through, to or from Darlington, reversed at Catterick Bridge. Traffic from the south had to reverse at Eryholme and again at Catterick Bridge to reach the camp. Nothing came of a proposal to add a southern connection at Eryholme, to form a triangular junction. The reversal at Catterick Bridge involved the engine running round the train. For convenience this procedure was usually carried out in the station under the control of the station signal box. If the operation was performed on the passing loop between the ground frame and Brompton Road signal box, the co-operation of the two signalmen was necessary. If it was required to keep either of the Richmond lines free for traffic, the running round was carried out on the military railway. In either case the train had to be propelled for a short distance.

Gradients on the line were steep and generally against engines travelling in the down direction from Catterick Bridge. There were considerable lengths of 1 in 40 and 1 in 46. Some time after 1942, improvements were made to the grading and in the course of these an 80 yard stretch of 1 in 27 was reduced to 1 in 50. Sudden reversals of gradient also occurred in places, the most notable being a short length of 1 in 59 falling in the middle of a 1¼ mile climb at 1 in 50, which commenced at the camp end of the Swale bridge. All locomotive classes were subject to an overall speed restriction of 20 mph, as the sharpest curve had a radius of 10 chains. Standard LNER cut-out speed restriction signs were displayed at Brompton Road and Camp Centre. It was also at these two locations that the Bordon influence was apparent in that some of the signals and chairs were of London & South Western Railway vintage.

The route of the railway left Catterick Bridge station and crossed Brompton Road by the first ungated crossing. Immediately beyond, on the down side, was the brick-built Brompton Road platform, together with the ground level signal box with its four-lever frame. This platform replaced the original one which was sited to the north of Brompton Road at the southern end of the yard limits. The earlier station layout was completed by a small booking office and a ground frame.

A falling gradient of 1 in 112 and 84 took the line past Farmers Arms crossing about 400 yards further on. The line then crossed the River Swale by a girder bridge, the only engineering work of any note on the railway. It was constructed by the Cleveland Bridge and Engineering Company, and consisted of three spans. A row of fire buckets was provided in case the wooden foot boarding should be ignited by cinders from locomotives. From this bridge a good view was obtained of the ancient, stone built, Catterick Bridge, carrying the Great North Road over the river a short distance downstream.

The original Brompton Road platform and signals close by Catterick Bridge station.
Author's collection

THE MILITARY RAILWAY: THE ROUTE DESCRIBED

The three-span girder bridge on the Catterick Military Railway over the River Swale looking towards the camp. Note the fire buckets. *P.W.B. Semmens*

The ground frame and signal controlling the Munition Works Junction within Catterick Camp. *Author's collection*

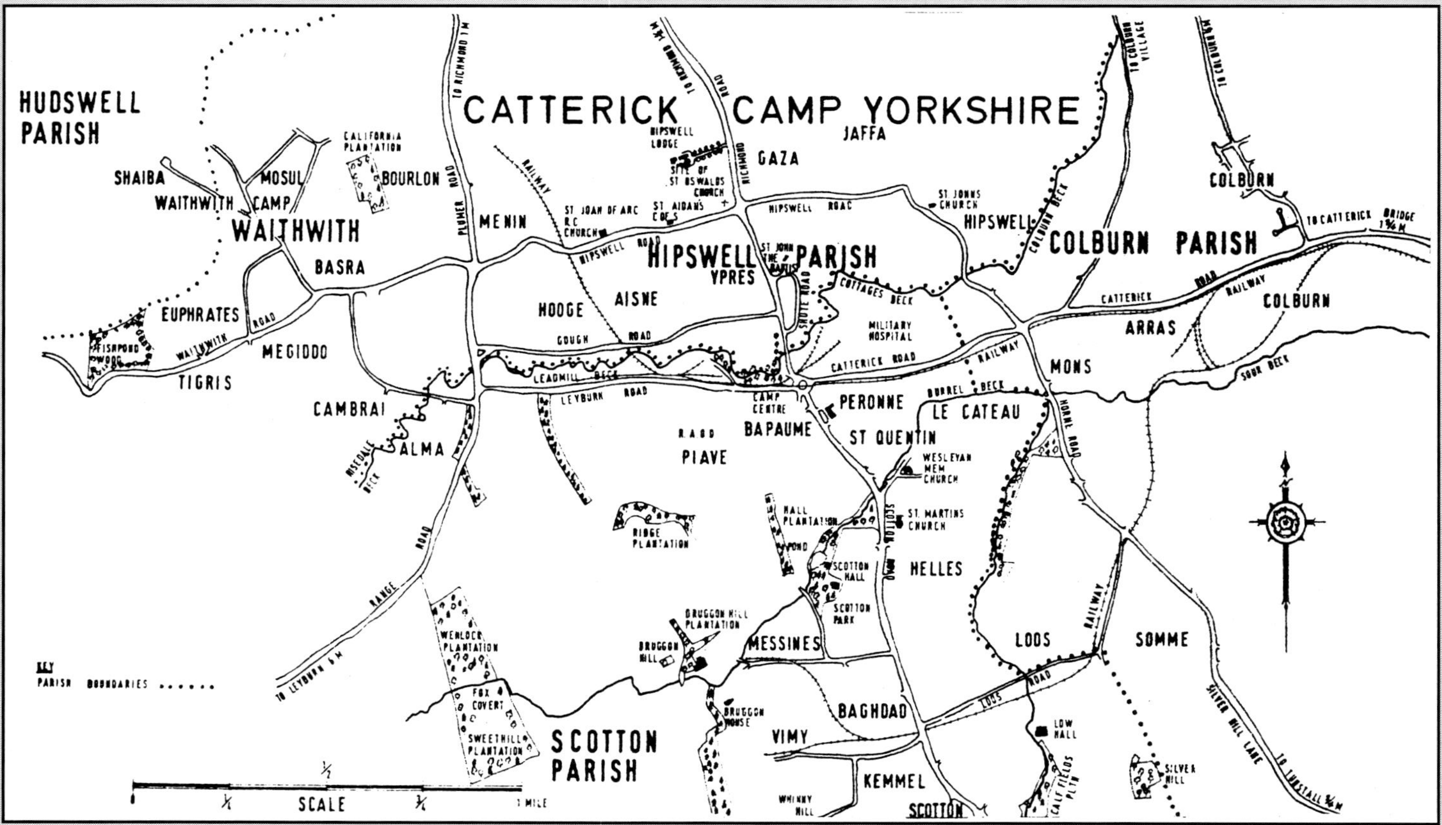

A map showing the military railway and also the location of the various lines within the Camp area.

Author's collection

The long climb mentioned earlier began immediately beyond the Swale bridge, the line taking a sharp curve to the right. The 1 in 50 gradient steepened to 1 in 46 at 1¾ miles. The line was provided with NER mile posts and 'whistle' signs were frequent. Two hundred yards further on Walkerville crossing was reached and the gradient eased to 1 in 85 shortly afterwards, before increasing again to 1 in 40 for ¼ mile at the 2½ miles mark. At Walkerville was Shed Junction, here was a two-road engine shed with facilities for major repairs, a water tower and a siding for the three-coach set of ex-North London Railway coaches plus two massive goods type brake vans, one of which was always at the rear of passenger trains. The locomotive headquarters were set up off a spur line to the east of the main line, the spur itself ran on for nearly a mile to the main stores.

Colburn ground frame was on a comparatively gentle 1 in 85 section, here was a passing loop and sidings serving an RASC depot known as East Depot; this was followed by a short down gradient at 1 in 73 and 84 near the end of the third mile. At Cinema Crossing the line continued to climb at 1 in 72 and 1 in 92 as far as Camp Centre station, just over 3½ miles from Catterick Bridge station. Camp Crossing was negotiated just before the platform was reached.

The brick-built station platform was situated on the up line of the crossing loop and faced the Military Hospital in Catterick Road. Little more than a halt, Camp Centre was nevertheless an important station,

The very basic facilities offered by Camp Centre station are evident in this photograph.
K. Taylor collection

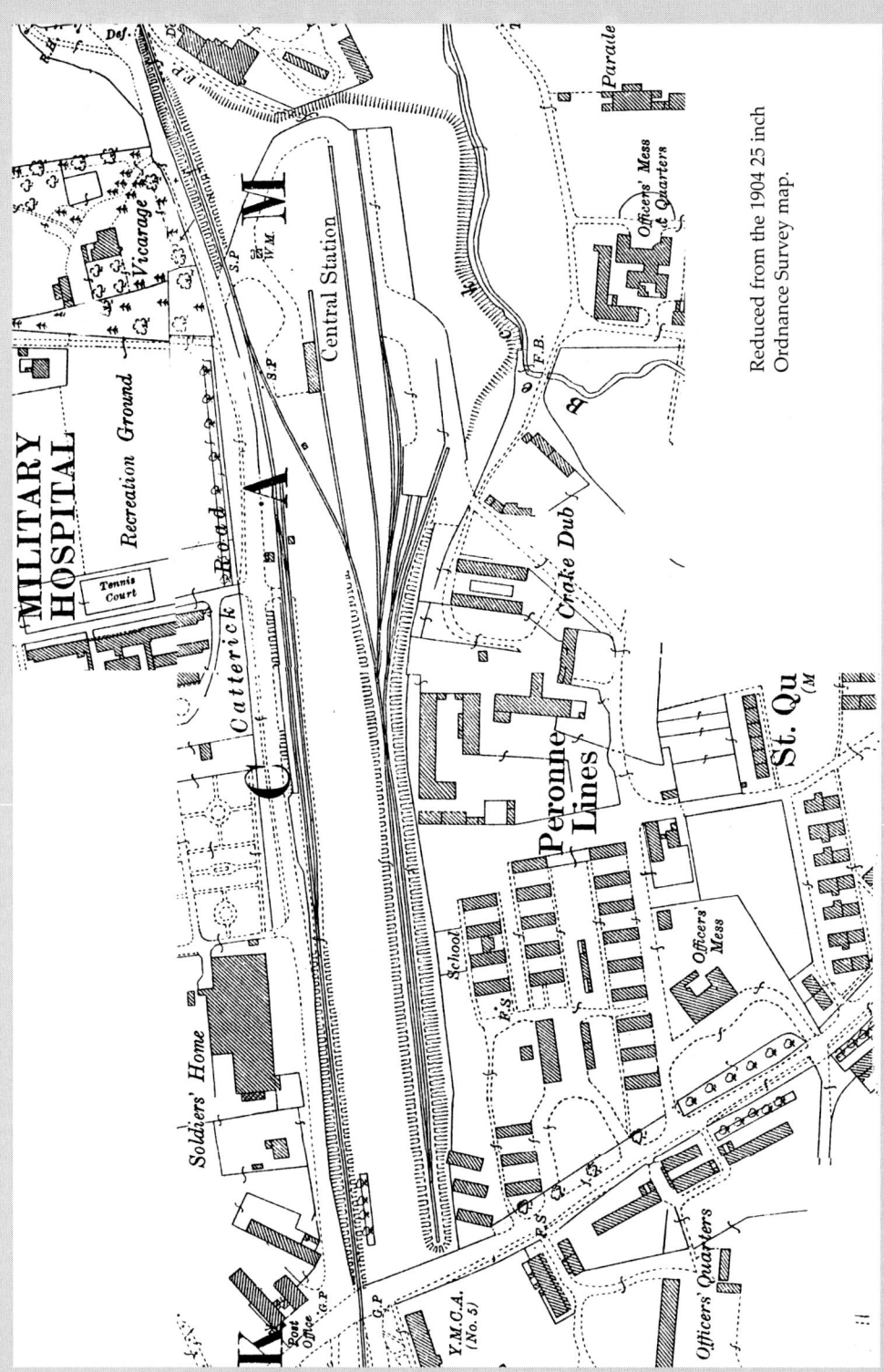

and very military. The station buildings comprised only a ticket office of red brick construction, 18 ft long. A large noticeboard proclaimed, 'All military personnel wearing civilian clothes will show their identity cards when purchasing tickets'. There was a long narrow platform with a number of concrete-bordered flower beds. It was from here that thousands of soldiers left Catterick Camp to start their journeys to the Far East, to India, the Mediterranean, in fact every part of the globe where the British Army saw service over the years following 1915. Here troops, together with horses and vehicles entrained; from here thousands left Catterick on their release leave, on their return to civilian life and thousands more crowded onto trains for 14 days' leave, 48 hours' leave, or a day return to Darlington.

Like the earlier platform at Brompton Road the camp platform was made of wooden sleepers until it was replaced by the brick structure in 1943, the work carried out by Italian prisoners of war; at the same time Brompton Road was relocated. There were locomotive watering facilities just west of Camp Centre station.

The line continued for another half mile beyond Camp Centre station, passing through the middle of a road roundabout en route to the power station sidings. Another siding served West Depot in Bapaume lines, recrossing the minor road beyond the road roundabout, by an open crossing. This depot had a network of lines.

LNER class 'K1' 2-6-0 No. 62005 at Camp Centre with an SLS railtour on 20th May, 1967.
H.B. Coulthard collection

In about 1960 a tender locomotive was derailed shunting the power station sidings. This was almost certainly due to the sharp left-hand curve on the line. In due course the breakdown train arrived and the engine was rerailed, only the leading bogie having left the rails.

The gradient on this section descended at 1 in 141 for 200 yards, the remainder rising at 1 in 42 and 1 in 63. Near the end of the line a trailing connection gave access to power house sidings. When the LNER took over the working of the line, passenger trains did not go beyond Camp Centre station. Prior to 1925 the line had continued beyond the power station, turning away to the west, over the moor to terminate at California station, just over five miles from Catterick Bridge and high above the Swale valley. A further spur went off from here, swinging away in a huge loop to end near St Oswald's depot. Soon after the LNER takeover, the track beyond power station sidings and shed siding were lifted.

The track throughout was laid with standard bullhead rails, the chairs, mostly LSWR and NER in origin, bearing dates from 1892 to 1900, in the case of the former, and 1905 to 1912, the latter company. Some of the North Eastern chairs were marked '90 Lbs' which could indicate the weight of rail used when the line was built. Although the line had the characteristics of a light railway all classes of locomotive were permitted to use it. It was also capable of carrying the large cross-channel railway guns.

The down home signal guarding the approach to the Camp Centre station yard on the Catterick Military Railway. The notice reads: *Unauthorised persons are forbidden to walk along the permanent way.*
A. Vaughan collection

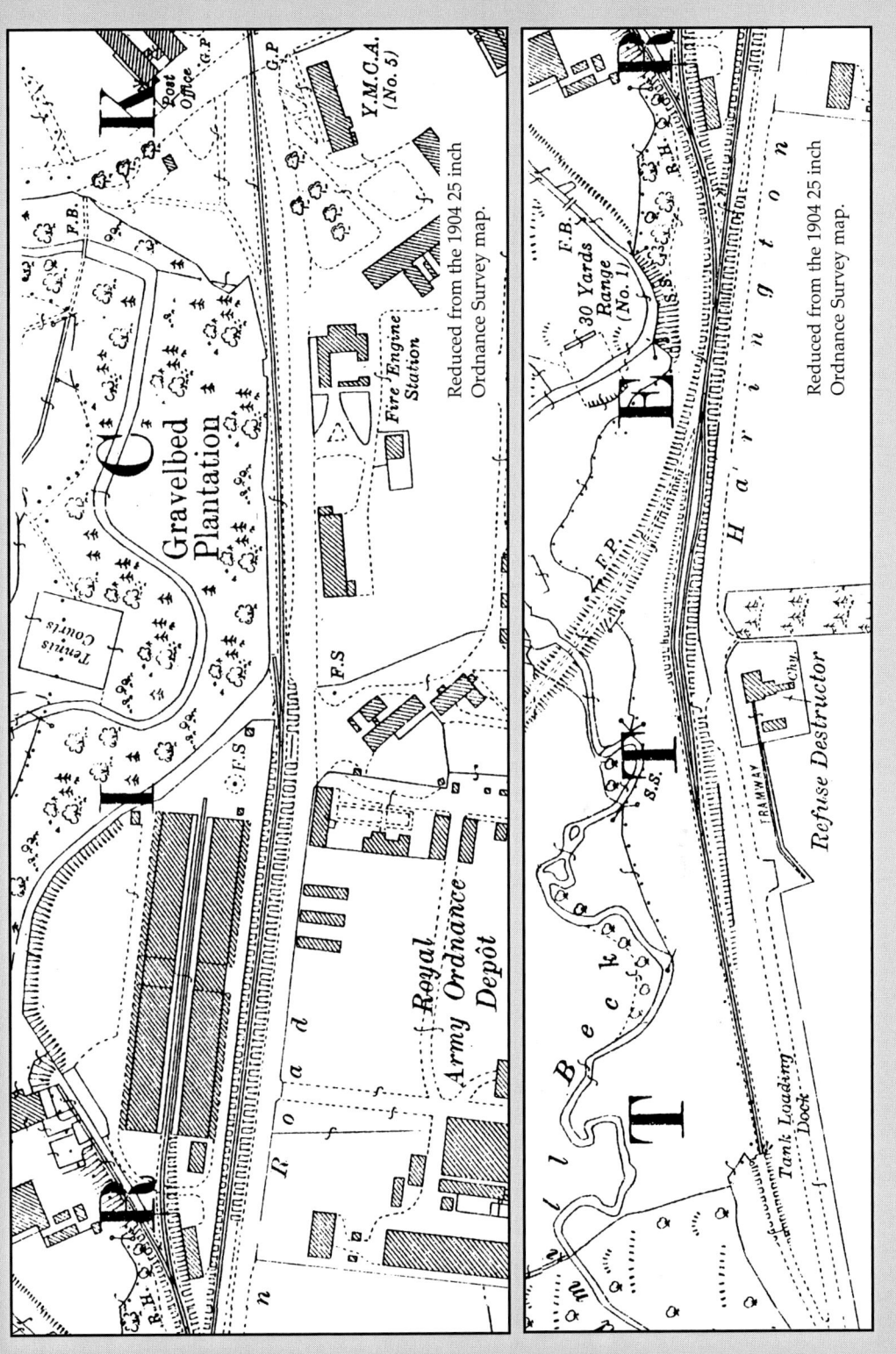

A busy troop train stands at Richmond station in 1939, with a well-loaded platform trolley in the foreground and the archetypal schoolboy on the extreme left. *Northern Echo*

GNR Ivatt Large, Atlantic 4-4-2 No. 4419 at Richmond with a train from Darlington. The engine is fitted with a locomotive booster, which runs from the cab to the smokebox. The locomotive booster was introduced in 1919 on the New York Central Railroad and allowed the trailing carrying wheels of a locomotive to provide extra power when required for starting on climbing gradients. Gresley was interested in fitting one to an Ivatt Atlantic because they were being stretched to their limit by increasingly heavy loads. By applying a booster to the trailing carrying wheels the tractive effort was increased by 50 per cent. The device was fitted to 1419 at Darlington Works in 1923. We see the engine possibly after an overhaul at Darlington in 1925. *J.W.Armstrong Trust*

Chapter Six

Catterick Military Railway Motive Power

With the completion of the military railway the War Department (WD) needed to acquire locomotives to operate the line. In 1916 the main line railways were running at full capacity and heavy engineering effort was being directed to war work, with the consequence that the War Department had to take what it could when buying in locomotives. Two typical examples of what was on offer were the Stratford and Midland Junction Railway (SMJR) 2-4-0Ts, Nos. 5 and 6. Built by Beyer, Peacock and Company, in 1885, these engines had 5 ft 6 in. diameter coupled wheels and 17 in. x 24 in. inside cylinders. The two locomotives had been on the SMJR duplicate list since 1902. Both engines were sent to Stratford-on-Avon in May 1916, for the WD to inspect them. They were accepted and £1,000 each paid for them. After repairs at Stratford costing £197, No. 5 was dispatched to Catterick and allocated the WD No. 94. In April 1918, the engine was generally repaired and fitted with a Westinghouse brake at Darlington, at a cost of £992. No. 94 worked both goods and passenger trains on the Catterick line. She was transferred to the Woolmer Instructional Railway in 1925.

Locomotive No. WD 94, 2-4-0T formerly the Stratford and Midland Junction Railway's No. 5. This engine worked both goods and passenger trains, often acting as a banker to No. 424. It is seen here on shed at Catterick Camp in 1921; also a good view of the water tank.

Author's collection

Ex-London and South Western Railway '415' class 4-4-2T No. 424. This engine was the pride of the line and dealt mainly with the passenger traffic. On the footplate is Sgt G. Drake and on the ground Sapper Hall, a steeplejack by trade. *Author's collection*

The local train on the military railway was fitted with the vacuum brake and was usually hauled by the pride of the line, a 4-4-2 tank engine purchased from the London and South Western Railway in July 1916. This engine was built by Beyer, Peacock, (No. 2176 of 1882) and was one of William Adams' standard '415' class suburban tank engines, having 5 ft 7 in. coupled wheels and 17½ in. x 24 in. outside cylinders. Whilst in LSWR service the engine carried the number 0424. Before arrival at Catterick it was overhauled by the NER, fitted with one of their standard safety valve covers and painted brick red with the '0' of its number painted out. All other engines on the Catterick railway were painted black. The engine does not appear to have been numbered in the WD list. No. 424 carried out prodigious feats with heavy troop trains on the grind up from the Richmond branch. If the load was too heavy No. 94 would pound away at the rear of the train. No. 424 was still in the shed at Catterick in March 1925 but may have been transferred to Erith depot soon afterwards.

CATTERICK MILITARY RAILWAY MOTIVE POWER

Three veteran saddle tanks used at Catterick were bought from the Rhymney Railway. These were six-coupled, outside-framed engines with 4 ft 7 in. wheels and 16 in. x 20 in. cylinders. Built as tender engines by Sharp, Stewart and Company (Nos. 2234, 2236 and 2238 of 1872) they were numbered 024, 026 and 028 by the Rhymney Railway, but by 1915 they were on the duplicate list. Nos. 024 and 026 were sold to the WD via Bute Works Supply Company, in November 1915 and June 1916 respectively. Given the WD numbers 100 and 101, they were sent to Catterick Camp. No. 028 was sold direct to the WD in June 1916 and, with the WD number 102, followed the first pair north. These massive saddle tanks mostly worked heavy goods trains at Catterick. At the end of 1921, No. 101 was transferred to Woolmer where it was scrapped in 1923. One of the remaining pair was sold to the Workington Iron and Steel Company, becoming their No. 52, until scrapped in 1928; this is likely to have been No. 102.

Six-coupled side tank engine, *Monmouth*, was built by the Hunslet Engine Company (HE No. 397 of 1886), and had 15 in. x 20 in. inside cylinders and 3 ft 4 in. wheels. It was delivered to the contractor T.A.

Locomotive No. WD 101, at Strawberry Hill on the LSWR, en route from Catterick Camp to Woolmer on 31st December, 1921. *H.C. Casserley*

Walker at Preston Dock and later moved to the contractors Price, Wills and Reeves, possibly working on their Immingham Dock contract. *Monmouth* arrived at the military camp at Cannock Chase in 1916. She was allocated the WD No. 86 and was transferred to Catterick in 1919. The engine was rebuilt by the Yorkshire Engine Works, at Sheffield, in 1923. During its time at Catterick *Monmouth* was used to shunt the exchange sidings with the NER at Catterick Bridge, occupying a small shed erected at the west end of the yard. In 1925 the engine was sold out of WD service through John Wake Ltd, of Darlington, to Carlton Main Colliery Company, for use at Frickley Colliery where it remained until scrapped in 1951.

A six-coupled saddle tank WD No. 104, was one of the 1350 to 1369 series built by R. and W. Hawthorn, Leslie and Company for the NER in 1875-76 (1668 of 1876), with 4 ft wheels and 15 in. x 22 in. cylinders. Three of these engines were sold out of NER service to John Wake in 1911 for £300 each. Repaired at North Road Works in October 1918, No. 104 (NER No. 1361) is unlikely to have worked anywhere else but Catterick during its WD service. It is likely that this engine was involved in the construction of the camp and during this time was based at Richmond shed. The engine was seen at Catterick in May 1924, for sale as 'Lot 17', it was probably scrapped at this time. Along with No. 103, 104 carried out shunting duties around the central camp area.

Locomotive No. WD 86 *Monmouth*, which was mainly used as the yard shunter at the exchange sidings with the NER at Catterick Bridge station.   *Author's collection*

CATTERICK MILITARY RAILWAY MOTIVE POWER

Locomotive No. WD 103 (originally NER No. 973) was a long-boilered saddle tank, rebuilt as a side tank in 1893, seen here in the company of Lance Corporal Burt, on the footplate and ex-NER fireman, Sapper Finlay, at Catterick Camp in the early 1920s.
Author's collection

Another NER engine was No. 968, one of two shunters disposed of to John Wake, which worked for a long time on the military railway, carrying the WD No. 103. This locomotive was originally NER No. 973, one of twenty (962-981) built by Robert Stephenson and Company to Fletcher's design in 1875, as a long-boiler saddle tank with 4 ft wheels and 14¾ in. x 22 in. cylinders. Put on the duplicate list as No. 1799, in 1869 it was rebuilt as a side tank at Darlington in 1893 and restored to the capital list as No. 968, corresponding in appearance with Worsdell's class 'E' (LNER class 'J71'). After Catterick this engine worked as *Neptune* at Milford Docks and was finally scrapped in 1947.

Locomotive WD 91, built by Manning, Wardle (1293 of 1895), was at Catterick at some point. This engine worked on the Stairfoot contract for W. Scott, moving to Whittaker Brothers, then to Belton Camp, RAF Cranwell, (both in Lincolnshire) and on to Catterick. It was sold to J.P. Edmonds of Stoke, and in October 1920, to the Sheffield Corporation for Ewden Valley Reservoir. Finally owned by Shanks and McEwan, Corby Steelworks, the engine, which carried the name *Don*, was scrapped in 1951.

A further locomotive was an 0-4-0 saddle tank, possibly Barclay No. 266 of 1884, sold to John Wake and apparently resold in 1917 to the Gas Light and Coke Company, Bromley. The evidence of the engine being at Catterick is rather nebulous, and it was possibly only there for a short while.

The service train on the military railway prior to the LNER takeover comprised three ex-North London Railway (NLR) four-wheel, four-compartment, (the compartment partitions reaching only to the top of the seats), close-coupled coaches. The centre coach of the set had its second compartment converted into a double-door brake compartment. The NLR supplied second-hand stock to more minor railways than any other company. Its stock was ideal as it was four-wheeled and designed for high density local work, with no frills and very solidly built. The coaches used at Catterick were of the second generation NLR type, having a slightly higher roof centre and raised lozenges on the doors. The two outer coaches carried the title 'Military Camp Railway' across the three spaces above the double windows between the doors. The door lozenges on the second compartment were lettered 'NCOs only'. The centre coach which contained the brake, was lettered 'MCR' above the centre set of double windows.

George Reed described travelling in the NLR coaches as,

> ... leaving odd, perhaps amusing impressions. The stock was known as 'Broad Street Bumpers', and to experience a trip in one of those sets left an indelible memory. The coaches were nominally four compartment, that is to say there were four doors each side, but there were no internal divisions so the coach was more like a van. Illumination was by two gas mantles which filled with water when it rained. With about half an inch of water in the bowl it caused a lens effect. The lurching progress of the vehicles caused the water to swirl about giving most striking distortions of greenish light over the interior and its occupants. Rhythmic puffs of acrid smoke entered each ill-fitting window and the effect of that, the lighting and the occupants bobbing up and down on the hard seats cannot be forgotten. Brake applications led to violent and noisy oscillation of the floor.

At the close of hostilities, in 1918, it was decided by the authorities that the camp was to become a permanent training centre. The camp railway became part of the LNER system after the 1923 Grouping and was worked by the types of motive power described in *Chapter Two*. Mr J.H. Price, who was at Catterick Camp in 1945, recalled the military railway trains as comprising, 'Three brown compartment coaches, some domed roof, some NER clerestories with those huge "electrified gas lamps", usually with some water and dead flies contained in the glass bowl'.

Chapter Seven

Operation of the Military Railway

Catterick Camp covered an area of approximately 25 square miles, and had as many as 45,000 men in it at one time. 10,000 passed through in the course of a single day and about 750,000 were dealt with in each year of the First World War. The troop traffic to and from the camp was exceptionally heavy. When the line opened seven passenger trains operated from Catterick Bridge station to the camp, the last two running right through to California station. Five ran in the opposite direction, plus an extra Saturday dinner time train, none of the return trips running from California station. On Sundays there were two trains each way between Catterick Bridge and Camp Centre station, and one, at 9.10 pm, through to California. Tickets were a simple roll type with 'Military Camp Railway' and the price printed on them, but no station name.

Goods traffic, bearing in mind the magnitude of the supplies required for so large a military population, was also on a considerable scale. In 1913 the NER dealt, at Catterick Bridge, with about 6,720 tons or 1,100 wagons; during the First World War the yearly average rose to 160,000 tons or 25,000 wagons. Between 1917-18 a special goods train was run

The military camp railway passenger set comprising three ex-North London Railway coaches and the ex-LSWR Adams 4-4-2T seen here in the vicinity of the camp's engine shed and showing clearly the livery of the line. *Author's collection*

every day conveying 60 or 70 wagons for the camp. In addition to the camp an aerodrome was built near Catterick village and the railway company dealt with about 350 aeroplanes and 3,000 tons of goods traffic annually in connection with it.

Although not specifically related to Catterick, the Railway Traffic Statistics relating to the First World War are of interest. These apply to the total number of special military trains run, men conveyed, together with the tonnage conveyed on behalf of the Government from the commencement of hostilities to 31st December, 1918, over the North Eastern Railway:

Number of special trains run	24,172
Number of Naval and Military passengers conveyed (originating in the North East only)	11,810,290
Number of work people conveyed	83,579.480
Number of horses conveyed	134,208
Number of vehicles, motors etc.	9,480
Number of vans of stores	43,204
Tonnage of Goods traffic carried on behalf of the Government and exclusive of 'through traffic'	5,524,989
Tonnage of coal carried on behalf of the Admiralty	1,975,693
Tonnage of coal from Durham and Northumberland collieries to London, 9 months ending December 1918	737,438
Tonnage of coal and coke carried to Cumberland (Coal Controllers re-organization scheme etc.) Increase 1918 compared to 1913	1,360,928

Locomotive Nos. 102 and 104 at the engine shed at Catterick Camp, also a glimpse of one of the WD wagon fleet. *Author's collection*

The Second World War saw what was the maximum service ever operated over the military branch. The timetable in force for the unadvertised Catterick Camp Military Railway trains during October-November, 1945 was:

WEEKDAYS		SO T	SO T	SO T			
Camp Centre	dep.	12.00	13.05	13.30			
Catterick Bridge	arr.	12.15	13.20	13.45	No Service Sunday		
Catterick Bridge	dep.	12.20	13.30	13.52	to Friday		
Darlington	arr.	12.38	13.50	14.10			
		SO C	SO C	SX C	SO T	SX C	SO T
Darlington	dep.	20.20	21.20	22.15	22.23	23.00	23.30
Catterick Bridge	arr.	20.46	21.50	22.33	22.41	23.30	24.00
Catterick Bridge	dep.	21.05	22.05	22.45	22.53	23.45	00.05
Camp Centre	arr.	21.20	22.20	23.00	23.08	24.00	00.20
SUNDAYS							
		C	C	T	T	T	
Darlington	dep.	20.15	21.15	22.30	23.30	00.20	
Catterick Bridge	arr.	20.45	21.45	22.48	24.00	00.49	
Catterick Bridge	dep.	20.55	21.55	23.00	00,08	01.00	
Camp Centre	arr.	21.10	22.10	23.15	00.23	01.15	

C - Change at Catterick Bridge   SO - Saturdays Only   SX - Saturdays excepted
T - Through train between Camp Centre and Darlington

J.H. Price remembered leaving Catterick for Germany in 1946. 'We were taken to Richmond by lorry to join a special train for Purfleet. The engine ran round at Eryholme Junction, we had a meal halt at Essendine then went on via Canonbury, Dalston, Victoria Park, Barking to Purfleet, thence by lorry to Tilbury Transit Camp and the next day to Ostend to Germany.'

Certain trains between Camp Centre and Darlington, notably the 22.30 and the 23.30 from Darlington on Sunday nights were combined with trains for Richmond and Camp Centre which divided at Catterick Bridge. A tank engine would be waiting 'round the corner' at Catterick Bridge station, the Richmond train would stop beyond the junction, the waiting engine would back onto it and take the last three coaches up to the camp. The front portion continued to Richmond. The later train on Sunday night might not go to Richmond but had six coaches for the camp. In this case the military branch engine would back on and the whole convoy, locomotive, six coaches, locomotive, would make its way up to the camp. It is unlikely that the military branch engine would have been able to cope with the train on its own over such steep gradients.

At times when there was no train to Camp Centre from Catterick Bridge troops would take the train to Richmond and walk to the camp from there. The stock for the first Richmond train of the day would stand in the south bay platform at Darlington all night and gradually fill up with (sleeping) soldiers changing from night trains.

At this time a daily push-and-pull service was operated on the military line to connect with trains on the Richmond branch. At Catterick Bridge these trains terminated at Brompton Road platform, only a few minutes walk from Catterick Bridge station. The push-and-pull service was operated by class 'G5' 0-4-4T No. 1837 and three coaches. Because of the long interval between issues of the Working Timetable these services did not appear in print until 22nd May, 1944. The push-and-pull service continued until 1947 but in the Working Timetable from 6th October it was dramatically reduced, leaving one Saturdays-only mid-day train to Darlington, and a return working in the early hours of Sunday morning. However some trains were eventually reinstated, particularly those carrying troops returning from weekend leave and reaching the camp in the early hours of Monday morning.

The reinvigoration of the camp railway during the Second World War saw the use of Darlington-based 0-6-0 or 0-8-0 locomotives working the camp lines; a class 'J27' 0-6-0 was provided to work heavy rail-mounted guns for testing and demonstration purposes. The passenger service between Catterick Bridge and the camp station was revived with trains running through from Darlington worked by class 'A5' or 'AB' 4-6-2Ts. The late night working mentioned earlier, involving a six-coach train, called for the use of two of these engines, another restored combination involved an 'A5' and a 'G5'.

The movement of military personnel continued to be a highly lucrative business for the railways, particularly from large camps like Catterick. There was keen and increasing competition from road transport towards the end of, and after, the Second World War. Some idea of the revenue earning aspect of the traffic is illustrated by the figure of £442,863, realised from furlough traffic at LNER stations during 1945. Catterick was served by a frequent service of connecting trains to most parts of the country, at Darlington. These facilities were augmented by weekend trains to London, Birmingham and Glasgow, with through return services from London, Birmingham and Sheffield to the camp station. In order to compete with road transport, reduced weekend furlough tickets to numerous destinations were available for travel outward each weekend and return at any time up to, and including, the following Tuesday. In 1954, the receipts at Richmond amounted to £65,291. Arrangements were made for railway staff to attend at the camp for the purpose of issuing tickets in advance to personnel going on leave.

British Railways noted in its Eastern Region report in 1956:

> The possibility that National Service will continue to be a feature of our national life and the recent announcement that Catterick Camp is to be modernised are indications that the military population in this area will remain high, and if properly handled, revenue from leave traffic should constitute a useful contribution to our coffers in the years that lie ahead.
>
> We should not lose sight of the fact that young national servicemen within our midst are the citizens of the future, and his judgement of our service will have a profound effect on his choice of transport on return to civilian life.

By 1952 the train service, apart from specials, consisted of a daily goods, a down passenger train, late on Saturday and Sunday evenings, and an up train at midday on Saturday, a Friday evening through train to Birmingham and four relief trains from Darlington in the early hours of Monday mornings. The latter trains commenced on 4th January, when the 3.30, 4.32 and 5.30 am reliefs for Richmond were diverted to Catterick Camp, and a fourth train introduced at 2.30 am from Darlington. There were correspondingly empty stock workings which were routed via Richmond. These trains conveying troops returning from weekend leave, continued to run in the early hours of each Monday morning until October 1964 and were latterly worked by diesel multiple units from Darlington.

The through Birmingham train was introduced in the late summer of 1951 and, in spite of not proving as popular as was hoped, it continued to run. This train left Catterick Camp at 4.28 pm and formed a useful leave train for troops heading for a weekend in the Midlands. Engines were changed at Darlington between 5.11 and 5.18 pm and the train arrived at Birmingham at 9.52 pm. The midday Saturday train was worked as empty stock from Darlington at 11.03 am; reaching the camp at 11.44 am. Returning at 12.35 pm it arrived at Darlington at 1.14 pm. The down passenger trains from Darlington were at 11.25 am on Saturdays and 11.40 am on Sundays. Except on Fridays and Saturdays, when it ran earlier, the daily goods train spent from about 9.00 am to anything between 12.00 to 2.00 pm on the military railway. Passenger loads at this time varied from three to five bogies of, usually, non-corridor stock.

During the late 1950s two trains departed from Catterick Camp, one on Fridays at 3.45 pm for soldiers with 48-hour passes, the other, on Saturdays at 12.27 pm for those with 36-hour passes. The times were rather tight, especially the Saturday train; most regiments had a CO's inspection on Saturday morning and no one left the lines until the CO had departed satisfied with what he had seen.

The Friday train ran north to Newcastle, London bound passengers changing at Darlington and waiting for a normal service train. The first was usually the 'Queen of Scots Pullman', but the excess fare on this train would have strained the finances of National Servicemen.

A Saturday train ran through to London, reversing twice in the process.

Two 4-6-2 tank engines were the normal motive power. They ran the train to Catterick Bridge, where they reversed the train into the up platform and then ran round via a second set of points beyond the level crossing at the east end of the station.

A remarkable photograph of rail-mounted 12" howitzers and their crews at Catterick Camp.
Author's collection

Any passengers travelling north left the train at Catterick Bridge and waited for the normal Richmond branch service to take them to Darlington.

The train then ran to Eryholme Junction, where a class 'A4', or similar, locomotive was waiting in a siding off the branch line. The train ran past the junction and onto the down line, stopping clear of the points connecting the up and the down line. The two tank engines detached and continued north towards Darlington whilst the 'A4' backed on at the rear of the train and eventually departed to York and London via the crossover.

The return fare to London for servicemen in 1955 was 36s. 8d., quite a lot to pay when recruits earned 28s. a week, only receiving £1 of that, the rest being accumulated either for use in long leave or to pay for breakages and losses of uniform. Servicemen were entitled to three warrants for free travel a year, these were saved for Easter or other longer holidays. For comparison, the return fare for civilians from Richmond to London was over £4.

Anne King, who was posted to Catterick Camp intermittently between 1954 and the early 1970s, described the return workings as being the most interesting:

> There was no reversing at Eryholme and the main train from London, the 11.55 pm from Kings Cross, ran direct to Darlington, stopping at York to pick up servicemen from the Midlands. Kings Cross was patrolled by Military Police, who turfed servicemen off other overnight trains to ensure that they used the special. Anyone in uniform or in mufti with an issue suitcase was easily recognisable, as were those wearing blazers with regimental badges.
>
> At Darlington the 'A4' locomotive departed and the two tank engines coupled up at the other end of the train. The short run back to Eryholme and on to Catterick Bridge was uneventful, the train being full of dozing soldiers, some the worse for drink. With some cigarette smoke thrown in, the atmosphere in some of the compartments was better imagined than experienced.
>
> After running round and backing along the down line clear of the points the train set off for the camp. Once on the steeper sections of the military line the fun began. On damp, misty nights, the wet rails caused slipping and the progress of the train got slower and slower. The carriage lights dimmed as the dynamos ceased to be effective, quite often the train would stall.
>
> There then occurred the usual business of getting up some steam, opening the regulator and simultaneously releasing the brakes. Release too soon and we ran back, release too late and the engines slipped, making a *feu de joie* of exhaust, and probably ejecting half the fire as well.
>
> Eventually the train crawled to the East Depot, where there was a level stretch. It was not unknown for sleepy soldiers to think that they had arrived

and try to get off the train. A few did get off to avoid a possible confrontation with the MPs, if their wrong doings over the weekend had gone ahead of them. The engines now blew up for a bit longer to raise enough steam to tackle the very nasty steep section just before the station. Finally with much slipping, and doubtless cursing, the train wearily dragged itself into the platform, both engines wreathed in steam but looking more like perspiration.

Here the passengers tumbled out and clambered into various 3 ton lorries waiting to take them to their lines. Within a few minutes the locomotives had taken water and run round. They then galloped off down the hill to Catterick Bridge. There was not much time to spare because another train from the north also came the same way, before or after the London train, depending on whether it was running late or not.

For any enthusiast with insomnia, the night's events could be heard with great clarity across the fields. The sound picture started soon after the train left Catterick Bridge station, every part of what I have described could be followed until the rake of empty carriages had hurtled down the spur. Of course on dry summer nights the slipping was missing but the climb remained as severe.

During this period the camp station was not used on Bank Holiday weekends. Instead half a dozen specials ran from Richmond station. At Easter, each travelling soldier was allocated to a train, and at some appointed time on Thursday, 3 ton lorries carrying those for a particular train would converge on the station and empty as fast as shouting MPs could arrange it. As soon as the train had gone, another waiting outside the station would be drawn in. This process continued for about three hours. Anne King remembers a short trailing spur just beyond the river bridge about half a mile from the station, 'I believe that the trains used a leapfrog system, with a spare engine taking out the first train, whose engine then took out the second and so on. The spur was probably the holding point for the locomotives, as the down line was occupied by empty carriages for subsequent trains.'

The departure starting signal at Richmond was of interest, because it had three dolls, one for the main line platform with an upper quadrant signal, one for the bay platform with a lower quadrant arm and a third small lower quadrant arm which controlled movement into what was possibly a locomotive spur, but whose extremity at this time ran into the up line. This was presumably to assist locomotive management on holiday weekends.

Goods traffic on the military line ran 'as required', and was possibly part of the Richmond branch daily pick-up goods train, although at times enough material had to be carried to justify a special train. Goods trains ran into the platform road at Camp Centre station, and when brakes on several wagons had been screwed down the engine was detached. Screwing brakes down was particularly important as the train was straddling the summit of the line at this point. The engine took water and ran round, and the train was split because if the full rake had been drawn back clear of the goods yard entry points, the train would have been on one of the steeper parts of the approach and the engine would have had trouble starting back up the incline.

Traffic for West Depot was assembled and the train ran through the station road down towards the road roundabout. Two shunters went ahead and stopped traffic on the road to allow the train to pass through the roundabout. The shunters performed a similar duty if the train was to shunt within the West Depot, which would involve crossing the road. For the run back to Catterick Bridge, the travelling shunters were dropped off before each road crossing to control traffic, and picked up when the train had crossed and stopped.

Steep gradients on the military line meant that wagons for the sidings at Walkerville could only be shunted off down trains and had to be marshalled as close to the guard's van as possible. Freight trains

LNER class 'K1' No. 62005 on the Catterick Camp branch with a steam special on 20th May, 1967 seen with an interesting collection of 'motorized' chasers. No. 62005 is now preserved on the North Yorkshire Moors Railway. *N.E. Stead*

descending the bank to Brompton Road were limited to 30 wagons, with one wagon in three having the brakes pinned down, additional braking being provided by a 20 ton brakevan. A class 'J25' locomotive was limited to 200 tons in the down direction and 270 tons in the up. Working instructions for the line indicated that, when freight trains were being run, the level crossings at Walkerville and Cinema were to be protected by railway lengthmen; the gates at Farmers Arms were opened by the fireman and closed by the Brompton Road porter-signalman in the case of down trains, and by the guard on up trains. With the passage of passenger trains over the branch, railway personnel were replaced by military personnel at Farmers Arms, Walkerville and Cinema. The camp crossing was always protected by the railway foreman in charge of Camp Centre station and Brompton Road by the porter-signalman from the nearby signal box.

The controlling of the various open crossings was the responsibility of the army. One of the most disliked duties was Railway Picquet; supplied by each regiment in turn it required about six men, an NCO and an officer. The Picquet's job was to man each open crossing when trains

LNER class 'A5' 2-6-4T No. 69842 arrives at Camp Centre station with an RCTS special. No. 69842 was the last of its class to be built in May 1926 and was withdrawn in 1958.
N.E. Stead

were due. During the day they carried a large red board bearing the legend, 'Stop train crossing', by night this was supplemented by red hurricane lamps. Three roads had to be manned, one at Catterick Bridge, one near the Walkerville Hotel and one at Mons lines where the Tunstall Road ran south. For the Friday departure, two men from the Picquet saw the first train away at the first crossing and were then picked up by a Land Rover to race down to the second crossing where another pair of soldiers were waiting to close their road. The first pair were whisked to Catterick Bridge to cover the minor road there. When the train was clear of the military line all the men were picked up, taken back to camp and dismissed until the time for the Saturday departure, when they repeated the performance.

Unless it was raining this was the better part of the duty. The worst was Sunday night and Monday morning. There were two trains to see up the hill to Camp Centre. At least they were travelling much more slowly and the Land Rover easily kept ahead. But for the men at the halfway point, two smelly hurricane lamps, a small wooden 'shelter', and stewed army tea from a flask were small compensation for a night out of bed.

The Picquet Officer had overall responsibility for the Picquet although the duty may occasionally have been carried out by the Garrison Orderly Officer. The officer had a second Land Rover and generally dashed about making sure that the men were awake and their red lamps lit; they also delivered tea at times.

During the latter days of the line, dmus provided the camp services until the closure of the Richmond branch to passenger traffic in March 1969; trains had stopped working through to the camp on 26th October, 1964. There was a lot of competition from coach operators who could have passengers in Leeds, York or Durham while Friday or Saturday trains were still shunting at Eryholme.

With the closure of the Richmond branch to passengers and the closure of the section between Catterick Bridge and Richmond station, freight traffic continued to run to Catterick Bridge until 9th February, 1970. Later that month workmen commenced to dismantle the military railway and the Richmond line itself, the work being completed between July and October, 1970.

During the line's busy history one serious accident occurred. This happened in the early morning of 15th September, 1917, and resulted in the loss of four lives and injuries to between 40 and 50 others. The accident involved the connecting train at Camp Centre station. The train was standing at the platform minus its engine, and soldiers of the Royal

Scots Fusiliers were in the process of boarding the train when it started to move off down the steep gradient in the direction of Catterick Bridge. Several soldiers managed to jump clear but about 150 remained on board. Reaching a speed estimated to be about 50 mph, the 120 ton train continued down the bank until the rear coach left the rails at Walkerville level crossing, becoming uncoupled at the same time. The remaining coaches continued until the second coach derailed and rolled down an embankment into a field. The coaches behind were either derailed or damaged. The leading coach continued by itself for a further two miles before it jumped the rails at the junction with the Richmond branch, hit some buffer stops and came to a stand on the ballast. The occupants of this coach escaped with cuts and bruises, except for one unfortunate soldier, Private Hugh Cameron, who upon alighting was run down by a train shunting on the adjoining line, and later died of his injuries. Two other men died in the derailed coaches and another in hospital.

The NER breakdown gang soon arrived to begin clearing the wreckage from the line. Evidence at the coroner's inquest established that at the time the line was being operated by the military, the signalman, guard and captain-in-charge were all in the Royal Engineers. In evidence the guard said that, on the previous evening difficulties had been experienced with the Westinghouse brake, but when he left the train in the loop at Camp Centre station he had applied four sets of handbrakes and chained the wheels of his brake van which he had not locked because he could not find the key. From the ease with which the coaches became uncoupled it appears unlikely that screw couplings were fitted. Handbrakes were fitted to some, if not all, of the coaches, but were found to be off after the accident, although no one could be found responsible for releasing them. One theory was that the tramping of heavy boots and the dumping of equipment caused that to happen, vibration gradually easing the brakes. The fact that they were off would mean that the train would begin to move as soon as the Westinghouse brake leaked off.

The train had consisted of 10 North Eastern six-wheel coaches; in the accident one first class and two brake thirds were totally wrecked. The others went to York Carriage Works, arriving 10 days after the mishap. All but one were condemned immediately leaving only brake third No. 22076 to continue in service.

Chapter Eight

The Remains of the Military Railway

My visit to the Catterick area to find out what remained of the railway took place on 14th March, 1992. Driving from Richmond the first obvious location point is the road roundabout at Camp Centre, through which the railway passed on its way to· its original terminus at California; in later days Power House sidings became the end of the line. This roundabout is now restored to a complete circle.

Within the confines of Catterick Camp (now Catterick Garrison), the site of Camp Centre station and the trackbed have been obliterated by Garrison Landscape Development, a landscaping scheme carried out between 1972 and 1978. A plaque on a rough stone obelisk standing adjacent to the road roundabout testifies that the scheme won a Civic Trust Award in 1978.

Although the station platform and buildings have gone, the low embankment upon which the railway ran, immediately east of the station, is preserved within the landscape project. The landscaping scheme continues as far as a minor path crossing the route of the line at Piper Hill. Beyond this point the course of the trackbed can be identified reasonably easily.

The road roundabout just beyond Camp Centre station which was bisected by the railway.
K. Taylor collection

The remains of the trackbed of the Military Railway as it rejoins the route of the A6136 road to cross over the A1 road. *Author*

The bridge which carried the Military Railway over the A1 road as it approached the crossing of the River Swale and Brompton Road platform. *Author*

The line crossed the A6136 road, with which it keeps close company for most of its route, at Walkerville; here the road has been widened thus obliterating any remains. The low embankment which carried the railway immediately beyond the crossing has disappeared but soon reappears as the line swings away from the A6136 in a north-easterly direction for a short distance, passing Ash House Farm.

The trackbed rejoins the road as they both pass over the A 1 road, the railway using a bridge constructed of steel supported on concrete pillars. A couple of hundred yards further and the line curves in a northerly direction as it approaches the River Swale. The impressive three-span girder bridge which carried the line over the river is still there. Although not usable as a bridge, in 1992, it served a useful function carrying various pipelines over the river. The bridge was reopened as a crossing in 2012.

A hundred yards beyond the bridge the line crossed a minor road opposite the Farmers Arms Inn, which is still open for business. Once over the road the trackbed is immediately occupied by a company selling caravans. The next crossing at Brompton Road (B6271) was the site of a platform which served the military railway. The brick-built platform survived until 1988 when it was demolished.

Beyond Brompton Road the line curved round to the west to join the Richmond branch, at Catterick Bridge station.

A view of the three-span bridge carrying pipelines across the River Swale. *Author*

Relics of the Military Railway preserved by Colin Stegeman. The relics were found during the construction of Colin's business premises close by the site of Brompton Road platform.
Author

Appendix One

Constructor's Locomotives

2 ft Gauge locomotives used by Harper Bros. & Co.

0-4-0ST o.c. Kerr, Stuart (2391/1915), new 4th May, 1915.

0-4-0ST o.c. Kerr, Stuart (2395/1915), new 8th May, 1915.

0-4-0ST o.c. Kerr, Stuart (2419/1915), new 12th June, 1915.
Later Premier Glynrhonwy Slate Quarry Ltd, Llanberis. Scrapped c.1931.

0-4-0ST o.c. Kerr, Stuart (2420/1915), new 21st June, 1915.
To Aubrey Watson Ltd, contractors. Later Billing Gravel Co. Ltd, Northants, then to Wraysbury Sand and Gravel Co. Ltd, Neepsend. Seen at Neepsend out-of-use in February 1948, it went to Sheffield and Rotherham Dismantlers for scrap in 1951.

0-4-0ST o.c. Kerr, Stuart (2421/1915), new 13th July, 1915.
To Daniel Davies and Son, Pembrokeshire.

0-4-0ST o.c. Kerr, Stuart (2422/1915), new 13th July, 1915.
To Aubrey Watson Ltd. Later East Midland Gravel Co. Ltd, Hunts. Scrapped c.1939.

All the above locomotives were Kerr, Stuart's 'Wren' class; known as the 'Old Type', they had inside Stephenson link motion and valves in steam chests above the outside cylinders worked by rocking levers. [The 'New Type' 'Wren' commencing with No. 2458 had outside Hackworth gear operating the valves directly.]

0-4-0WT o.c. Hudswell, Clarke (1160/1915).
To John Dickinson & Co. Ltd, Bolton, Contractors, named *Billy*. To Stone and Hutchinson, Bolton, possibly for scrap.

0-4-0WT o.c. Hudswell, Clarke (1161/1915).
To A.H. Price & Co., Nottingham. Later Harold Potter & Co., Nottingham, dealers.

These two engines were built for the account of Robert Hudson to War Office Order and delivered to Harper Bros., 'Richmond Camp', on 29th June, 1915.

0-4-0T o.c. Avonside (1593/1910).
This was new to Pensford and Bromley Collieries Ltd, Somerset but was transferred early in 1913 to Old Delabole Slate Co. Ltd in Cornwall, from whom Harper acquired it in February, 1915.

Standard Gauge

0-4-0ST o.c. Manning, Wardle (780/1881), WD 98.
This was new to Lucas Aird, Ackworth, its later history, prior to Catterick is unknown. May have gone from Catterick to the Sheffield Coal Co. To NPF Hackney Wick. For sale June 1921.

Appendix Two

The Armoured Trains

The construction of the first armoured trains to be built for use in England during the First World War was a demonstration of co-operation between four railway companies. The gun trucks carrying the trains' principal armament were Caledonian Railway vehicles, the infantry vans were supplied by the Great Western Railway and the Great Northern Railway (GNR) supplied the engine. The assembly of these units was undertaken at the Crewe Works of the London and North Western Railway.

The locomotive chosen for the first train was GNR class 'N1' 0-6-2 passenger tank No. 1578, built at Doncaster in 1912. Armouring was carried out at Doncaster Works and involved protecting the entire engine, above and below the footplate. The engine's condensing gear, which allowed it to work through the Metropolitan tunnels to Moorgate, was retained. The armoured engine weighed 72 tons with a maximum axle loading of 19 tons 14 cwt. The infantry vans were marshalled at either end of the locomotive and a 12 pounder quick firing gun, which had proved its worth in South Africa, was marshalled at each end of the train.

The engine selected for the second armoured train was No. 1590, another 'N1', this time coupled to an old six-wheeled tender of the Stirling era. This train, like the first, was assembled at Crewe and when completed, in 1915, was dispatched to St Margarets locomotive depot, in Edinburgh.

Although they were under military control the armoured trains had civilian enginemen detailed to work them, and the working instructions provided that in the event of the

Armoured train engine of the Great Northern Railway class 'N1', 0-4-2T No. 1578 seen here at Doncaster in December 1914.   *National Railway Museum*

trains having to undertake active war duties, the men would at once be enrolled in the army. This entitled them to treatment as soldiers in the event of capture by the enemy.

Armoured Train No. 1 was intended to assist in the defence of the coastal regions of Norfolk. It was known to have visited Great Yarmouth and to have operated on the Mundesley branch. Armoured train No. 2 stationed at Edinburgh, was within a few miles of the Forth Bridge, regarded by the military as the most vital and vulnerable of targets for possible enemy attack. During its wartime service Train No. 1 acquired the name *Norna* (sometimes described as *Norma*, however, photographic evidence during the train's sojourn at Catterick Camp shows the former spelling to be correct). Train No. 2, was named *Alice*.

The armoured trains were taken out of service as soon as the war ended. Both were seen at Peascliff, near Grantham, in June 1919. During the same year the engines, at least, were at Catterick Camp, 'Norna' under the charge of driver Chaistell and fireman Gibson. Nos. 1587 and 1590 were sold back to the newly formed LNER in 1923, taken to Doncaster for the removal of their armour and returned to work on the London suburban services. They continued in service until withdrawn, within a few months of each other, in 1956.

Armoured train, *Norna*, at Catterick Camp about to be broken-up after the First World War.
Author's collection

Appendix Three

Mechanical Cab Signalling System

A mechanical cab signalling system developed by Vincent Raven for the NER was probably the first successful attempt at a comprehensive cab signalling system. It appeared in 1894 and was eventually installed on 46 miles of the NER.

A later, electrically operated, development of this system appeared in 1905. This was a unique system in that it repeated, in the engine's cab, the aspects of the running signals. It consisted of several bars situated between the running rails at equal distance between the approach side of the distant and the stop signals. A spring loaded shoe was fitted below the locomotive, between the leading wheels. When the shoe came into contact with a bar it transmitted an electric current to receiving equipment in the driver's cab. This consisted of a dial and a bell. The dial repeated, by means of a miniature semaphore arm, the attitude of the running signals in advance. Route information was provided by a pointer moving to either of two positions depending on the route set. The pointer remained upright if no junction was involved.

A bar, situated 150 yards on the approach side of the distant signal, when passed over by an engine, caused a bell to ring in the cab as a warning to the driver of his approach to a signal, it also activated the miniature semaphore to the upright position.

If the running signals were in the 'Off' position, the bell would stop ringing when the engine ran over the bar at the distant signal, the miniature semaphore arm was lowered and the junction indicator moved to the appropriate position.

If the running signals were showing 'Danger', the bell continued to ring at each bar and the miniature semaphore arm was placed in the horizontal position. If the running signals were lowered before the engine reached the intermediate bar the bell would cease ringing, the miniature semaphore arm lowered and the route indicator deflected to the appropriate position.

If a train was brought to a stand at the home signal and the signalman wished to draw it forward past the signal at 'Danger', for the purpose of shunting or to move forward to the starting signal to await acceptance from the box in advance, the signalman, by pressing a small switch on his instrument, caused the miniature semaphore arm in the engine cab to move up and down as a signal for the driver to pass the signal at danger.

The main fault with the Raven system was that it did not apply the train brakes. On 4th June, 1910, authority was given for the system to be installed on the Richmond branch at a cost of £900. This included the fitting of the apparatus to 15 engines. The system was brought into use on the branch on 14th August, 1911, and only engines appropriately fitted were allowed to work the branch. The practice seems to have fallen into disuse after the First World War.

Front cover: Ivatt Class '2MT' 2-6-0 No. 46481 enters Scorton station with a passenger train on 1st June, 1951. No. 46481 was one of a class of 128 engines introduced by the LMS in 1946 and were the first really modern steam locomotives produced in Britain for many years. They were ideal for branchline working. *J.W.Armstrong Trust*

Back Cover: Upper - Class 'A5' 4-6-2T No 69842 ,the last of the class to be built,. stands at Catterick Camp station with an RCTS Special on 11th October, 1952. *J.W.Armstrong Trust*
Lower - Class 'A5' 4-6-2T No. 69835 arrives at the Richmond platform at Eryholme station with a passenger train on a winter's day.The line off to the left led to the Darlington Rolling Stock Company,which repaired wagons. *J.W.Armstrong Trust.*